RONALD A. KERN

LOVE YOUR WORK

Unlock Your Potential
Love Your Life

Love Your Work
Unlock Your Potential, Love Your Life
Ronald A. Kern © 2019

Print ISBN: 978-0-9965361-1-0
eBook ISBN: 978-0-9965361-2-7

Interior and Cover Design by: Fusion Creative Works, FusionCW.com
Lead Editor: AnnaMarie McHargue

For more information, visit RonaldAKern.com

Published by
TH Publishing

Printed in the United States of America

This book is dedicated to my late mother, Kay Kern, who taught me (by example) how to be caring, compassionate, loving, forgiving, generous, and many other important life lessons. She was a remarkable mother, teacher, and friend. I miss her terribly since she went to paint the skies in Heaven in 2013. She was also the first person with whom I shared my goal of writing a book. She had no doubt that one day this book would be written. Mom, I hope you can read this in Heaven.

Table of Contents

"99% of failures come from people who make excuses."

—George Washington

"Life's most persistent and urgent question is, 'What are you doing for others?'"

—Martin Luther King, Jr.

"It is better to offer no excuse than a bad one."

—George Washington

"To be good, and to do good, is all we have to do."

—John Adams

"Work as if you were to live 100 years. Pray as if you were to die tomorrow."

—Benjamin Franklin

Introduction

So many of us spend our lives chasing the American dream and accumulating material wealth. The point of this book is not to discourage this behavior but instead to encourage and inspire you to do so by following your passion, whatever that might be. What I have learned over the years is that we are happiest when we love what we do and help others while we do it.

The challenges to be successful on your chosen path may seem insurmountable at times, but when you are tenacious and doggedly pursue a life that includes your greatest passions, the rewards are endless.

What follows are not just stories and encouragements from people who learned and are living these great truths, but lessons you can learn from, implement, and grow—both personally and professionally.

Meet Ronald Kern

Although he was $26,000 in debt and had no formal education after high school, he founded a private investigation company in the basement of his parent's home. He and his wife, Lisa, turned it into a multimillion-dollar operation and one of the top five firms in the United States.. It, as well as his multitude of other businesses, were sold in late 2013, allowing him to pursue other ventures at the age of 44.

Ron has a column in *Christian Living* magazine, writes for several other publications, and loves writing about personal development and business principles that work.

With no formal education after high school, he has spent years earning certifications that help his clients such as personal development, leadership, communication, coaching, training, confidence building, goal setting, and psychological mindsets. Combined with his 25-plus years of business experience, he understands the measure of success is based on results and he helps his clients create those results.

It is his desire to use his experience and resources to encourage, teach, support, and equip his clients with actionable, real-life, and sustainable tools that work. Ron wants to help you unlock your potential and strengths.

He is considered an expert in life transformation and personal development and a business and entrepreneurial guru.

Ron attributes his success in life and business to the never-ending support of his wife, Lisa, a lot of hard work, and his faith. Ron and Lisa have been married 28 years and in late 2018, they sold their dream home and now live on a 42-acre piece of paradise they call Back Forty Farms. Back Forty Farms offers equine assisted trauma care, cooking classes, natural produce, and much more.

Working for Others: Ronald Kern

(Husband, Father, Entrepreneur, Author, Speaker, and Consultant)

There was a time when I felt the universe revolved around me—what I said, what I did. Long before Facebook or Twitter, I had a large network of people who helped me spread my news quickly. I did well in high school, was voted class vice president, excelled in tennis, and was "one of the guys." I did what I wanted, when I wanted. High school truly was for me a collection of glory days.

And even though I tried to heed my mother's advice to "be kind to others," I was never consistent. It was the Ron Kern Show, day in and day out, almost all the time.

As I headed into adulthood, much remained the same. I did well with one of my first jobs and climbed the ladder quickly. After a year of winning a few awards and breaking some company records, my office became a "shrine for Ron Kern." I mounted plaques, clipped magazine articles, framed photographs with top executives. My walls screamed, "Look at me!" At the time, those awards were how I gained validity, self-worth, and comfort. "If you don't toot your own horn, who will?" I thought. For years, this was my modus operandi. *Look at me.*

But then a few things started to shift. My eyes began to wander. I started recalling my mother's words to be kind to those around me. That it wasn't all about me. And, with God's help, my focus started to shift away from myself and toward those around me.

Talk about changing my life exponentially! Not only did my wife and I begin to flourish in our personal life, but we also began experiencing unparalleled growth in our business. All because I finally saw that serving others with intent, purpose, and wise discernment was the only true key to fulfillment.

God helped me turn things around. Whether or not you are a believer, though, this book has many treasures to help you learn and grow. The verses that follow, for example, are encouraging to anyone looking to understand the beauty in servanthood, regardless of your spiritual leanings.

Mark 9:35: "And he sat down and called the twelve. And he said to them, 'If anyone would be first, he must be last of all and servant of all.'"

Galatians 5:13: "For you were called to freedom, brothers. Only do not use your freedom as an opportunity for the flesh, but through love, serve one another."

Mark 10:45: "For even the Son of Man came not to be served but to serve, and to give his life as a ransom for many."

But what does it mean to serve? I frequently say and firmly believe, "If you are being blessed, it's so you can then be a blessing for others."

This doesn't mean give away all you have worked hard to get, as that would be silly. God wants you to enjoy these blessings. Instead, it is my hope that this book will offer stories to encourage you to see the value in serving others. Originally, I thought it might be fun to tell the stories of one or two people who discovered joy in service. But as I started talking about the concept with others, God brought innumerable people into my life who had beautiful stories to tell. My short book turned into a collection of valuable life lessons all with the theme of giving back to others.

If you want to have a fulfilling, successful life, help others. Do it without fail, without reservation in your heart, and without expectation. If you do it in this manner, prepare for something incredible and life-changing.

We all have gifts, talents, and blessings to share with others, regardless of our financial position. Whether it be a smile, food, a warm coat, kindness, assistance, wisdom, experience, or the most precious gift of all, time, we all can be a blessing to others (#beAblessing). There is no reason to withhold a helping hand.

I do realize that we can't help everyone, so give with discernment, but also realize that "when someone has been given much, much will be required in return." (NLT Luke 12:48) When you start giving, you will start to notice gifts—and unintended sources of joy and happiness—coming toward you from all directions.

It took me a while to understand these keys to happy living. In fact, it took decades. It is my hope that *Love Your*

Work will help launch you on your own path to happiness far more quickly!

When our investigative business won the Idaho Small Business of the Year in Meridian, Idaho, I thought I'd be addressing just a few people in a place the size of a coffee shop. I was surprised to see about 250 professionals there, including the mayor, business owners, and others looking to me for wisdom on how to run their businesses.

One thing you don't do at a gathering like that is talk about God. Being politically correct, as we all know, is a must. Keep things general. Don't offend.

So after setting the stage, I immediately broke the rule and pulled God in. I went bold.

"Decisions, both large and small, should be prayed about. In fact," I challenged them, "email me in six months and let me know what happened, how your company was affected positively after praying genuinely." You probably guessed that no one emailed me.

I said other things that day that were less important, but I shared that a part of me was curious and inquisitive; not necessarily in an intrusive way, but interested in understanding how all things fell into place.

In 1986, I watched a movie about a bounty hunter, and my interest was piqued.

I ended up going to work for Target as a security guard, where I searched for and arrested shoplifters or employees who were stealing from the company. It was a game of cat and mouse, catching the bad guys and sending them to jail. I was good at it, doubling both the number of apprehensions and the number of internal thefts discovered. Not only was I learning a lot, I loved the work. We'd come a long way from when we were first married, but God wasn't done providing us blessings.

After a few years, the criminals started to know who and what I was—and I knew who they were. When I began to fly around the country investigating criminals in the company, people knew my purpose. "Uh oh, Ron's here . . . who's going to jail?"

While I was doing well and had gained the respect of my colleagues, something in me stirred. Dealing with the corporate aspect of things fueled some discontent. I knew quickly that I wanted to be my own boss, even if it meant leaving behind a steady job and income. I'd always had an entrepreneurial spirit, so I pondered what I could do on my own. Soon after, with just a card table and computer, I launched an investigative business: Kern and Associates.

I knew very little about the investigation business, so with dial-up internet I researched nonstop, trying to learn a job I'd never done before. I also read books and talked to anyone who'd offer advice. Sometimes I stayed up all night, doing my research, knowing that to succeed in business, I literally had to pour myself into it. With zero college and zero education in my chosen field, I didn't have the luxury to just sit back and hope it all worked out. My complete lack of business sense and experience didn't help much either.

Kern and Associates got a few little jobs, here and there. In the first year, it netted $700, and I was ecstatic. While I learned more and more about the P.I. business, I was still working at Target full time.

It was while Lisa was pregnant with our son, Tony, that she really started getting involved. I was still Kern and Associates, but she felt a name change was in order. That day, Shadow Trackers, Inc. was born.

Soon after, we had a call from a man whose dialect I'd never heard before. I told him, "You sound like you're in a tunnel or a tin can or something." He told us he was calling from the back of his limousine in Saudi Arabia. Stunned, I asked how someone like him had found a business like ours; one that barely even had a web presence—not to mention we were located in Boise, Idaho. He told us he'd seen the name, "Shadow Trackers," and liked it.

This would be just one of many examples of when Lisa's input was so right, so accurate. Like the name change, her input, support, and vision were critical to our growth.

Our new (and first international) client told us of his son, who was in the U.S., and asked us to help find him. He'd been through a nasty divorce; his ex-wife had the kids, had remarried, changed her last name, and hadn't kept in touch. He'd been looking for them for almost 24 years. We found them in seven hours, which was like lightning back then.

The grateful Saudi client said, "How much can I pay you?"

Although I believe you should be compensated for your value, we didn't even take any money for the job. The fact that we were successful was payment enough for us.

He sent us a heartfelt letter, telling us about how his life was now fulfilled, having rekindled the relationships that meant so much to him, after looking for them for so long. I still have the letter to this day.

Finding them had been pretty easy—maybe this career was something we actually could make a living doing.

Eventually, the whole story was sent to Oprah, but also was picked up by the *Washington Times,* the *New York Times,* and then *Family Circle* magazine. The ball was rolling, and we were still just operating out of the basement. When the most-watched local news channel interviewed us, (me in my trench coat and fedora, for effect), it continued to enhance our presence. After that the media became even more interested.

Before we knew it, our name was everywhere and business began to boom. Our business exploded to the point where we had to hire employees, then more employees, then more. We had to design and implement systems into our business not only to keep up but also in order to grow without losing quality.

We were in magazines, newspapers, television shows, and more. I thought the pinnacle had reached the absolute highest point possible when I was chosen as one of "The Leading Private Investigators of the United States," which appeared in *PI Magazine.*

Lisa began learning the fine art of the background check, while I continued to work on my investigative skills. I needed to gather as much experience as I could as quickly as possible. We learned that our business oftentimes forced us to deal with a few shady characters. Once an angry man tapped his gun on my car window, vowing to "take care of me" if I continued to follow him on a surveillance case.

Meanwhile, Lisa was also beginning to do civil process serving, where she was getting "experience" of her own. She hoped those she was serving had heard the phrase, "Don't shoot the messenger," but at times she doubted it. Someone did something wrong, and someone was getting sued, and they typically weren't very happy. They'd been notified again and again, and had been avoiding the consequences. Many who'd been actively evading being served required sneaky dinnertime, 10 p.m. or Sunday "surprise servings," but even still, there were those who knew how to play the game. Some would openly lie, saying, "They don't live here," even though they were the very person being served.

Others thanked Lisa for being discreet and not making a scene. But, of course, those were the exception. As someone who is non-confrontational, quiet, and reserved, she had to grow thick skin and learn how to draw the line, especially when she was being chased by men carrying lead pipes or golf clubs, or worse, when someone set their dog loose on her.

She also had to make her way through small rural cities or neighborhoods known for their staggering crime rates. To say they were dangerous wouldn't begin to cover it. In those places, it was common for us to serve together, but often time limitations forced her to fly solo. She'd frequently been told that her naiveté kept her safe.

That naiveté and niceness worked for her. Her best defense was how nice she was to people, no matter where she went, be it the grandest home in a rich part of town or the shack lean-to style some called homes.

Not only was her work hard on a number of levels, it also involved a lot of driving, as she was eventually serving hundreds of papers a day. Long before GPS technology was available, Lisa had to create daily driving plans, without the benefit of detailed directions. Some days she'd hit Burley, Wendell, Jerome, Bliss. She'd line them all out, hit one town, and then go on to the next town.

While my regular job at Target didn't interfere initially, it was getting to be a lot to juggle, and we were coming to a crossroads. Being the visual person I am, I put the pros and cons of leaving my steady "real" job all down on paper. I hoped this would offer us a clear answer.

Even without Shadow Trackers, Inc. having employees, rent, or other business expenses we didn't even know about, on paper we could see instantly that leaving Target would not work for us financially. We now had two kids, a car payment, and had just bought our first home. Everything about quitting Target said, "No, no, no." It hit hard when I realized I would be working for someone else indefinitely.

Always the optimistic person, Lisa brightly said, "Well, what if it *does* work?"

I shook my head. "What if it doesn't?"

Lisa said, "What if it does?" and I quickly replied again, "What if it doesn't?"

She was so positive and optimistic it was starting to rub me the wrong way. In my mind, there was no way.

She asked, "Three months from now, are we still going to be going back and forth about this?"

She continued to challenge: "Do you want to be 80 years old, sitting in your rocker, wondering, 'what if'?

"You've always asked for answers and have received guidance," Lisa told me, "and when has God ever let us down? Plus, you can always go get another job."

I decided to ask God for guidance. This was, after all, one of the most important decisions for the company's future—and ours, for that matter. The idea of quitting my job to follow my passion was terrifying. I kept imagining my family with no money, no food, and homeless. I needed a little more nudging before taking the plunge. It wasn't that I expected God to send me a burning bush, but I was asking Him to give me a clear, unambiguous sign.

Not long after, Lisa's grandfather paid us a visit. I'd never had a grandfather, growing up, so Jerry Mercer was my grandpa. He was highly intelligent and had been instrumental in my walk with the Lord. He'd pastored and mentored thousands in his lifetime, and on anything relating to the Bible or God, I considered him an expert. Like my mom, Grandpa constantly encouraged me to be more involved in my relationship with God. As soon as he walked into our new home, we hugged, and then he immediately looked over at our den, which doubled as our office, and he said, "When are you moving out of this and getting yourself a real office?"

To be so abrupt was unlike him; he wasn't at all one to say such things, yet it was the first thing out of his mouth. It was out of the blue and odd.

It was the sign I needed. Also, I could not stop thinking about what Lisa had said repeatedly: "Do you want to be 80 years old sitting in your rocker wondering 'what if?'"

I put in my two weeks' notice at Target. There was no looking back. I was so excited over being able to devote myself full time to Shadow Trackers, Inc. but scared all the same. Fear is tricky—it can be either a motivator or a roadblock.

On a whim, we drove down Main Street in Meridian, Idaho, to see a 900-square-foot office space even though it was far larger than we thought we would ever need. Money was tight, but we had ourselves a storefront.

With so much space, we discussed hiring a couple of people to help. For years we'd worked 10-, 15-, or 18-hour days, together or alone. Long nights were typical. We were thankful for the work, but it became a tedious grind. We eventually hired employees to do the serving for us.

Before we knew it, we had filled the place with employees, as more clients came our way.

After several years, we moved to a 1,300-square-foot office, the front portion of a large building. When the owner offered us a ridiculously good deal on the offices in the back of the building, we took it. This move put us right back where we started; with tons of empty space. We figured that God must be working! The space wasn't empty for long. Like an army, whenever a tenant moved out of the huge building, we'd take over, and then outgrow what we had. Blessings continued to flow.

Before we knew it, we had outgrown every square foot of that building . . . this time to a 10,500-square-foot building on Main Street. By that time, we had almost 50 employees, and we'd never have to move again.

With growth came a lot of change, but one thing that never changed was our viewpoint about how to treat employees. Wanting so badly to ensure that our ethics and morals would never be jeopardized, we might have been overly fair, and even overly kind. Maybe we would have grown faster or gotten much bigger without those guidelines in place, but had we lessened our resolve, individuals could have been lost in the shuffle or clients might not have received optimal service. That just wasn't something we wanted. We wanted to be known as a company that provided excellent service, gave back to the community; we wanted to be an organization that blessed others.

One day, after landing one of our biggest clients, we were going full steam. We were responsible for handling nearly 80 percent of Ada and Canyon County servings, and served from Burley, Idaho, to Ontario, Oregon, and everywhere in between. Between 1999-2006, we easily served 10,000 or more.

Times, however, were changing. More often, our people were being put in jeopardy. Things started getting crazy. Our servers were getting spit on or were being threatened as angry people jumped onto their cars. Add to that, gasoline prices were at an all-time high. It became painfully clear that we would need to part ways with some of our largest clients because we could no longer serve papers. We knew immediately that this was the right thing to do.

Not serving papers anymore allowed our background check and surveillance divisions to be even more of a focus.

Sadly, we did a lot of surveillance for women wanting us to track their husbands' movements. Some had been married for anywhere from 20 to 36 years. We'd follow those men and observe them holding hands with other women. Sharing this news with their wives was awful enough, but worse yet was their inability to believe what they saw in pictures. They wanted to see more before considering it "proof." As if the dagger wasn't in deep enough, now they wanted to twist it.

At that point, we'd tell them, "Look. We will not take your money to go prancing into a hotel room. Here is the truth: Your husband and the other woman are more than just friends."

In their hearts, they already knew that.

It was one of the things that separated us from other places who would do anything for a buck; we never wanted to do anything we'd regret.

We started to get awards for the cases we were solving, and those were nice. Beyond that, as the owners, we still didn't get a lot of pats on the back for a job well done; we were never the "employee of the month." While many larger companies had HR people and accountants for taxes, bookkeeping, payroll, insurance, and keeping employee files, I had Lisa. With no specialized schooling, no training, she taught herself to do it all, and she did it amazingly well. In retrospect, she handled alone what should have been at least three employees.

Most of our motivation continued to be internal, knowing we were doing the right thing. But sometimes, I'd pause and ask myself, "What do *we* get?" My ego was starting to show its ugly self again.

My work at Target catching bad guys had been very ego-driven, but as business owners, pats on the back or words of encouragement were rare. I still needed recognition for my work and successes. That is, until I became a parent and something shifted. The need to tell the world how great I thought I was gradually disappeared. Knowing in my heart I'd contributed to the greater good was becoming enough; I no longer needed trophies on the shelf or brownie points. One day, I packed up all of them up and donated them.

Somewhere along the way, I realized that no matter what you do or how hard you work, someone's always going to be better, smarter, prettier, and more successful. It's a tough pill to swallow, but it's a fact—regardless of the profession, school, or area in which you live. My wife puts it another way: "If you allow your happiness to be dictated by external people or circumstances, you'll be disappointed every time, as eventually all will fail you. Happiness is how you respond to adversity, and happiness truly comes from within." This is not just a cliché and if you get serious about what she said and try to live it, your life will change.

My thinking on so many things began to shift over the years. As far as satisfaction goes, I learned that growing from making that $700 in the first year of business to grossing several million dollars a year didn't feel much different. I also felt, as my kids were getting older, that my real joy came when I helped to develop others. I'd been teaching, training, and guiding our employees, and it was paying off. Once I helped them develop in their roles, I was able to watch them grow. The small part I played in that brought me joy.

Sometimes I'd step out for a week or so and then try to step back into the Shadow Tracker's mix. I noticed my presence actually hampered things, messed with the flow. One day I was even told by our operations director, "You're not really needed. Go home." She was very blunt and honest, but I swallowed my pride and knew she was right. Upon my return, I'd walk in, ready to save everyone, put out any fires, and get the company back on track. To both my dismay and satisfaction, our business not only survived but actually flourished during my absence.

One thing was clear: We'd arrived. I wish I could say it was because of my intellect, or from all of my higher education, but I firmly believe it was a combination of God and this: If you have a goal, if you have passion, if you are persistent and put that passion into action, if you are willing to look fear in the eye and still move forward, you'll surprise yourself by your own drive. You will not only make it, you will far surpass your initial goals.

You must understand, realize, and know this: the only person who can get in the way or has the power to stop you from succeeding is yourself.

When I rewind my memories back to those years, when I was driving 100 miles a day with Shadow Trackers, Inc., I was gratified to know that I hadn't missed any plays, recitals, or games for my children, but still I wondered how many times I'd bypassed other moments because I was trying to satisfy a particular client or finish just one more thing. That's just not the way to do it. There will be other opportunities, other businesses, but there is never going to be a second chance to raise your kids. You can start over with almost anything else, but not with them. You get one shot. They'll appreciate, adore, and love you, or they'll resent you.

We sold the company on October 31, 2013, and "retired."

Wondering what to do next and with options wide open, I took a closer look at what we as a couple really loved to do. Fighting for the underdog always brought me satisfaction. There are people out there who just need to be heard and cared about. God's words, "I will bless you . . . and you will be a blessing," continued to ring in our ears.

We'd been trying to do that through our business for years. And we knew we would do the same for the next 20.

It was time to leave our comfort zone and figure out how we could help, how we could make a difference for those around us.

We were ready.

WHAT'S YOUR ACTION?

Meet Lisa Kern

Lisa Kern has managed the finances of all companies that she and Ron have owned, including a private investigation firm, a real estate holding company, and Ron's current endeavors with consulting and product sales.

She also helped develop and launch LIMBitless, Inc., a nonprofit for the adaptive and wounded veteran community. Each year, LIMBitless helps amputees and those who are paralyzed or suffer from brain injuries or other physical trauma to challenge their limitations and overcome obstacles in their lives, both physical and perceived.

Lisa has a passion for nutrition and health. She loves to cook and plans to open a facility on their ranch in which she can teach others about the joys of food and how to nourish not only their bodies, but also their souls.

Ron and Lisa have been married for 28 years, have two grown children, and reside on a beautiful 42-acre farm in Idaho, where they hope to continue blessing others in many ways.

Give Without Expectation: Lisa Kern

(Wife, Mother, Entrepreneur, Chef, and Gardener)

Ron and I met while we were both working at the Holiday Inn in Boise. I'd only planned to stay in Boise for a few months, since I was going to school at Washington State and was just there between semesters. Ron was working as a disc jockey in the bar, and I was working pool concessions for the summer. He'd heard talk of the "new girl" and when he saw me come into the bar to get drinks for guests; he accidentally let the music end. He went home and told his mom about me, saying he didn't think he had a chance.

Ron's mom said, "Ask her out. What's the worst that can happen?"

He had a friend fold napkins into roses, used fruit from the bar for garnishes, and delivered the entire bouquet to me. Then he asked me for a date. When I said yes, he said, " . . . Seriously?"

Our first date was supposed to have been one of two rafting trips, organized by our employer. As it turned out, I had chosen one date, Ron the other.

He tried again. When Ron drove over to pick me up, he got lost.

When we finally connected, we became inseparable. We held hands and were giddy, smiling—basically sickening to those around us.

Six months later he took me up in a friend's airplane with his dad as pilot for a flight over Bogus Basin ski resort. On my first plane ride ever, Ron proposed to me, and I said yes.

People asked Ron what he was thinking, proposing so soon. They told him he didn't know me well enough, that he should go to college and then get a good job before considering marriage. They said it would never last, and that we weren't ready. Ron disagreed, and so did I. We believed then, and continue to believe today, that following your heart is not only a good thing, but so much more fulfilling than simply doing what you think you are "supposed" to do.

We got married. We had children. We started Shadow Trackers, Inc., where we worked for over 15 years. We kept the business for another five, even though we knew the company was no longer our passion. And we now know why: The people who were meant to buy our company weren't ready yet. They, too, were following a dream and their timing had to be right.

Ron and I signed the papers and went home. That very night Ron said, "I'm unemployed," followed immediately by "I'm bored."

"Here we go again," I thought.

If Ron had remained the same sort of person he was when we first got together, he might have fallen back into the trap of chasing materialism. As much as I loved him, he tended to be on the egocentric, cocky, "my way or the highway" side.

But over the years, things changed. His priorities shifted. He began to see his success and his move from getting by to wealth was far more spiritual than anything else. We went from low-income housing and government cheese to having more than enough. During those years, he also gained something more: humility. He no longer needed to wave a flag that said, "Look at me!" Ron says he attributes this change to feeling the spirit of God.

When he began Kern and Associates, (later renamed "Shadow Trackers, Inc."), I figured it was just a little hobby thing, that he'd do it, get tired of it, and stop doing it.

Then he got business cards. He did a bunch of research and found out where to get the answers he was looking for. Being a total type A personality who requires very little sleep, he was completely obsessed and did everything possible to make his business work. If Ron gets his hands on something, he's going full out with it, no holds barred. He has that drive; he has that kind of passion.

I watched him working long, 18-20-hour days for years as he learned a lucrative business from the ground up. He'll tell you now that he did everything the hard way, the long way, being new to the business. I think he did it just right.

We look at each other and say, "Without you, it wouldn't have happened." We came to the realization that we make a good team. I don't happen to have a personality that's hugely motivated, but I'm steady. Ron has that constant drive to move forward. We worked together to make the investigative business thrive.

We want to tell people about the blessings we've experienced. While others might view it as tooting our own horn, we have a strong desire to share the fact that we stepped out in faith to start our business. We might not have had abundance during those early years, but every need was provided for, and we didn't go hungry.

During the time we ran Shadow Trackers, Inc., our net revenue exceeded that of the previous year, every year—21 years in a row. The income that first year was $700; near the end it was seven digits. We spent only about $1,500 in advertising from start to finish. Very few companies can tout that kind of success.

I share this with you *not* to brag but instead to share a point.

If you have passion and put it into action, have faith, and bless others in the process without expectation, you will be abundantly rewarded beyond your wildest imagination.

Read back the statement in bold. Burn this into your mind. If you take something away from this book, it's the above. Don't forget that statement. Do it. Live it. Enjoy it.

Never once did we look back with regrets, or say, "We shouldn't have done this."

So screw up. Make mistakes. Live your life. That's how you learn where your passion lies.

For the last five years we owned the business, it became evident that Ron had trained enough good people to run it without him. You'd think that would have been Ron's goal, but in truth, it left him feeling lost. It was hard for him to give up that control.

Eventually, though, he went back to his roots and recalled what his mother had always taught him; that he should treat others the way his mother did, to find ways to help where he could.

We wanted to put a name to that.

During a cruise we'd taken years before, our ship made a one-day stop in Roatan, Honduras. The place stuck to Ron over the years. We loved it there, but the poverty and conditions were heartbreaking. Later, we took our son and daughter on a similar trip, wanting to share what we'd found with them. As we were leaving Roatan that day, we all agreed that we really liked the place and wanted to spend more time there.

A couple of months later, we began looking for Roatan real estate and found a business for sale. We spent a week exploring the island and making lots of connections with the people there. During that week, we went into the communities and noticed that, education-wise, the children were sadly lacking. We left the island with no business and no residential property.

When we got home, we mentioned to a friend that Roatan was a place of great need, the sort of place that could really use some help. Somewhere that would benefit greatly from a ministry. Ron was all over it. Within a few hours, he had a company name and logo, had designed and published a website complete with photos, and was putting together the first project. It felt exactly like when we started Shadow

Trackers, Inc. We had no idea what we were doing but we just jumped in with both feet.

Ron made all the contacts, did all the research, and set it all up just like he's done before. We both determined that instead of sending help over, we were going to be on the ground, delivering supplies. We didn't want to be absentee helpers; we wanted to attend to the work at hand. We wanted to be the blessing for others, whether they were five miles away from us or halfway across the globe.

If you asked anyone, a year before this happened, if they could have pictured Ron or me selling our company and starting a ministry to devote much of our time, energy, and resources to traveling the world and spreading the word of God and love of Jesus, no one would have believed it.

We'd never done anything like this before; we would normally just send a check to WorldVision and leave it at that. I never pictured either of us being that kind of person. But we've learned that God doesn't only call the equipped, He equips the called. We're taking that same philosophy and drive we had with our business and putting it toward the ministry. Little by little, we're learning what we need to learn, and he's putting the people and other ministries in place to help us.

You know how these things go. You have grand ideas, and God says, "That's not even close to what I have in mind." For us, that's the way it's always been. We've tried to be "nice" to people and have attempted to help others. Sponsoring a family at Christmas, giving back in some way. But this? This is on a much larger scale. Who would've dreamed it would go this way?

So we're making the trips, and the spirit is changing our lives. We're hugging the Roatan kids, learning Spanish, taking Christian Education classes to become associate pastors and learning all about nonprofits.

Ron sets big goals. We're talking about sponsorship programs where people can leave Honduras, get their education, and return to Roatan to make a difference. He thinks big, which makes the rewards big, and in this case children who truly need it will be the recipients.

We get to see some of the faces and witness the immediate effects of what we're doing. But we can't do it for that reason. There will be many we've touched, more often than not, that we'll never know about; we may never hear their stories. So we'll do the work, and let God handle the details.

WHAT'S YOUR ACTION?

_____

_____

_____

_____

_____

_____

_____

_____

_____

_____

_____

_____

_____

_____

_____

_____

_____

Meet Dan Rusanowsky

Dan Rusanowsky was born in 1960 on New Year's Eve in Milford, Connecticut, about 20 miles south of the Canadian border.

Interested in the performing arts early on, each week he watched Jackie Gleason and the Ed Sullivan show on TV. He admired the way they entertained people and were so quick on their feet. He loved what they did and thought he might like to do the same.

At age 10, his uncle took him to a National Hockey League game at Madison Square Garden. He fell in love with the game. Since most games were only available on the radio, he soon also fell in love with radio. His drive to find a way to be involved resulted in an announcing and broadcast career.

Dan produced 18-plus seasons of broadcasts for the Sharks, with his usual broadcast partner, Jamie Baker, or on occasion David Maley, and sometimes with both in what they called a "triple-cast." Rusanowsky is San Jose Sharks Radio Network's operator and administrator and had the honor of calling the NHL Game of the Week on Westwood One Radio Network.

On March 21, 2004, he called the Sharks' 1,000th game, and called their 1,300th game in 2009. On January 16, 2018, he called his 2,000th regular NHL game with the Sharks against the Arizona Coyotes.

For us, he Kern family addiction to hockey began when our son started roller blading in our cul-de-sac, which led to neighborhood hockey games. Someone told me if I tried playing ice hockey, I wouldn't ever stop. He was right; I have played for seven years. My son played high school hockey and travel hockey for the Junior Steelheads. My daughter even played goalie during her high school years. Then, as a family, we started watching NHL, went to Idaho Steelheads games, and began to cheer for the San Jose Sharks. Then we decided to catch a game or two or a hundred at "The Tank" where our Sharks worked their magic. We became certifiable, raging fanatics with Sharks' gear overtaking our home. Hockey, we learned, was an experience, not a game.

Communicate Your Passion: Dan Rusanowsky

(NHL Hall of Fame Radio Announcer/Voice
of the San Jose Sharks)

Like any American boy during the late 60s and into the 70s, I liked baseball and also hockey, growing up so close to Canada and experiencing NHL games at Madison Square Garden. During the memorable summer of 1973, the Oakland A's came to my state to play the New York Mets in the World Series. The Mets, who'd been in last place, took it all the way to the World Series, right up to Game Seven. I listened nonstop to the radio, where Bob Murphy called the Mets games.

I followed hockey in the winter and baseball in the summer, and lived it all through the magic of radio. The fact that the reception wasn't ideal, creating static, only piqued my imagination by making things more interesting, enhancing the experience. I admired Gene Ridell, the Rangers' number one center, because he was a highly skilled, classy hockey player. I really admired Bobby Orr but hated to see him playing "my" team. When I did get to attend a game in person, it was just that much more exciting. I started imagining how I might get involved.

As a teenager, I watched the area's NHL Rangers' games on our TV with its snowy reception, having to position the "rabbit ears" antenna just so. When it came to games, more choices were available on the radio. KMOX St. Louis with Dan Kelly, the Blackhawks and Lloyd Pettit, and Bruce Martin in Detroit doing a Redwings game could all be heard on air at night. I began passionately following the game of hockey.

Playing some hockey in high school helped me understand what it was like for other players. I knew I'd started the sport too late, so I decided to just enjoy it.

We didn't have a rink in my hometown until I was about 15, so I got a job, paid for my own equipment, ice time, and everything. I also enjoyed the performing arts and performed in a few plays but wasn't comfortable with the drama club group—and by that time, sports had taken precedence.

I began attending Yale hockey games with the same uncle who took me to my first game. Coupled with the hours spent listening to the radio, I got a good dose of the hockey life.

I knew I didn't have a voice like, say, John Miller's baritone. I'm more of a tenor. One of hockey's greatest voices, Foster Hewitt, is also kind of a tenor. I also knew that more people were interested in broadcasting other sports, and that hockey was probably the hardest to broadcast. For a beginner, the barriers to entry were smaller in hockey.

Back then, the likelihood of getting a visa and going to Canada to do play-by-play, when the Canadians were all doing that, were slim. There was no reason for them to hire an American. That left about 24 U.S.-based teams (i.e., 24 jobs). With 300 million people in the U.S., and one me, I knew my odds weren't the best, but I didn't want to have any regrets; I had to try. But how could I break in?

I felt the answer was to get the best education I could, learn a lot of different skills, and be able to do many different things. That way, if radio didn't pan out, I wouldn't be 30 and jobless. I looked around at so many who were trying to become doctors or stockbrokers for the money, yet I wanted to follow my passion.

"Do what you like, and the living will follow."

Choosing a college wasn't about the money, for me. This was my thinking: I could go to Syracuse University Newhouse School of Communications, the place that produced Bob Costas, Hank Greenwold, Dick Enberg, and on and on. The problem was everybody in my entire class at that big school would want to do the same thing I wanted to do. Getting hands-on experience would've been extremely difficult right up until I was maybe a senior. I wouldn't get enough experience there to get started.

Or, I could go to another school, like St. Lawrence in Canton, New York, where they had both a Division One hockey team and a radio station. It was very good academically, had great alumni, was a terrific place to live, and only had 2,500 students.

The plan was to call games in this order: Division One hockey, then the American Hockey League, then the NHL.

I showed up, walked to the radio station at the school, and approached the guy that did the play by play. I said, "I want to do what you do. I want to learn from you. Is that possible?"

He said, "Yeah, it is. As a matter of fact, we'll take care of getting you some space in the press box, and you get a tape recorder and microphone. Practice calling games as if you're on air, and we'll listen to them. There are one or two games at the end of the year where I may have a scheduling conflict. If you're good, we'll let you do them."

I was thinking, "This is fantastic!"

When I recorded a kind of pre-season exhibition game a couple of weeks later, he listened and said, "I think you have some potential for this. I think by the time we get to that stage of the year, there's a really good chance you might be able to do the game. I have one guy who might do it, but I don't think he has the same interest level or breadth of knowledge."

When we'd first met, I talked with him a lot about college hockey and how I'd been following it closely for years and how I'd gone to the Yale games. So he knew how I felt about things.

That next week, the first game of the regular season, St. Lawrence was playing Harvard, and it was a home game. The sports information director was the caller, while the guy from the radio station did the play-by-play. At intermission, the sports director left the booth to deal with news media and any problems with the team. This left the play-by-play guy in charge of intermission.

Sometimes during intermission, they played taped interviews, and sometimes they hosted live guests or they'd go back to the studio for news. That first intermission on that first game, the play-by-play guy walked up to me and said, "I've got a scheduled interview for this intermission, a writer from *The Hockey News*. You're going to have to do the interview. I can't do it."

I said, "Why can't you do it?"

I asked why, and he said he had to go to the bathroom, and it was his only chance to go.

"Here's the mic," he told me. "This is Tom Burke. Tom, Dan Rusakowski's going to be doing the interview. Thirty seconds, you're on air. See you later."

To this day, I'm still not sure if he really did have a bathroom emergency or if he'd just planned to test me. In this job, the technical part of it is that you have to know how to react to things quickly.

There were a couple of things I shouldn't have done, but we got through it.

When he got back, he told me, "Everybody said it went well, no problems. I think you can come with us on a road trip in two weeks. The sports information director has more work to do down there. We're going to Brown, New Hampshire, and Boston. You can do color with me."

On that trip, a guy's head hit and broke the glass during the very first game at Brown. They didn't have a replacement pane and had to send someone across town to get one before the game could go on—it took 26 minutes. And there are no commercials. So, we just talked about the college hockey world and what was going on. It really was something—a special experience where proved I could do it, that I could actually handle it. I was 19 years old at the time.

I began to learn the radio business, too. The school had two stations: the current one, and the NPR station. It had a more professional air and professional staff, but sometimes they let students do things there. They began having me do intern-like stuff, but then said, "You know, you can be on the air."

It was basically a classical music station. I did their Sunday mornings, starting at 6 a.m. and going until 1 p.m. I took the crappy shift because nobody else wanted to be up that early on a Sunday. It was a lot of fun. I learned more about classical music, learned about editing tape for news and how to execute a radio broadcast, and I got work-study money. So it became a paying job.

Lesson learned? You can't be afraid to ask. I had to go out, take a deep breath, look someone in the eye and ask them. St. Lawrence was a good decision. I got on-the-job experience, earned some money, and also got a great education.

Of course, there were barriers to entry: I was young. I was immature. I didn't know the industry well enough. But I took full advantage of the opportunities presented to me and along the way, created a few of my own.

By the end of that first season, I did three games on my own. It was great practice and experience.

By my junior year, I was doing all the games on a professional radio station because the school had moved from the NPR station to a station in town. Again, I was going through some of the same age and maturity issues, so I really had to earn my spot. But for a 21-year-old, things were going pretty well.

I was also writing a column for the local newspaper, which was even more exposure for me and helped the team.

We ended up on a couple of the commercial stations, and I got involved with some talks with them, again because they needed someone who was passionate and interested. People seem to be drawn to that kind of passion.

When I first started, St. Lawrence was the worst team in Division One. By my senior year, the team went to the NCAAs and played a couple of games in Madison, Wisconsin, winning the National Championship that year.

We helped turn that team around.

Once I was done with school, I still fully expected to call games in the American Hockey League, but there were no jobs open. I wasn't sure what I was going to do. I wasn't crazy about uprooting and going to the International Hockey League and to a place I knew nothing about.

So when an opportunity came to call games for Clarkson, Saint Lawrence's cross-town rival, I was torn. Clarkson and Saint Lawrence hated each other, as both were very good Division One teams.

I just couldn't make myself go to the Clarkson games. I attended grad school there but kept going to St. Lawrence games. I got my MBA, learned a lot about the business world, and never took my eye off the ball (or in this case, the puck). The summer of my graduation, there were four or five American Hockey League job openings. I didn't, however, get the job I thought I'd get.

Instead I was offered a position in New Haven, my home area, where I would provide radio play-by-play for the New Haven Nighthawks. I lived with my sister for five years and was able to make it all work, even though it turned out to be very a challenging situation, business-wise. But that experience got me to the point where I was ready for the NHL. The team I worked for was owned by the L.A. Kings, but I knew there wouldn't be any opportunities for me in L.A.— the guys doing the job had been there for years and likely weren't going anywhere.

Then . . . an opportunity.

Everybody was interested in San Jose, because it was a brand-new expansion team with no agendas or people from other organizations who wanted to hire who they wanted to hire. I sent my tapes in just like everyone else, and I got the job. I've been calling their games for 28 years.

I've been able to do a very special thing, being part of this team from the beginning, from the ground up. At one point, we had a 17-game losing streak. But the Sharks were determined. They worked their way up and have made the playoffs for the past 10 years.

My path worked for me. The passion I kept burning during my MBA years has benefited me all this time. In San Jose, I have been part of the business side, even putting together the radio network for the team, and so I used all my business skills.

The American Hockey League was a huge part of my life. I learned everything I could about the hockey business, about how difficult it could be, and about the challenges faced by every team.

We used to have three games in three nights. We played Friday night at home, and Saturday night if we won. We'd get to the arena about five-thirty, play the game, leave the arena around 11, get some sandwiches, get home at two, and then have a five o' clock game the next day. It gave me a lot of respect for the players who were tough enough to handle the grind. Many couldn't do it, and they weeded themselves out. The rest used their passion to set themselves up for success.

The other part of it was that if you're financially motivated, it's a much slower process for earning a good living than people think. Once you make it to the NHL, it's a good living and a good place. It's extremely fulfilling.

The team hasn't won the Stanley Cup yet but did win the conference championship in the 2015-16 season.

Knowing that I have built my career doing what I love is more than satisfying. I awake each morning and am so happy to get to do my job. It's not because I make a good living, it's because I am living out my passion. Chasing the dollar wouldn't bring me any of the joy I feel.

Everyone has a special talent. Life's all about discovering what that is for you. Find out what it is, and then don't give up. Pursue it and enjoy your life, because the journey is far more important than what you have. If you follow what you're passionate about, your life will be everything you could hope for.

WHAT'S YOUR ACTION?

_____

_____

_____

_____

_____

_____

_____

_____

_____

_____

_____

_____

_____

_____

_____

_____

_____

_____

Meet Ivan and Beth Misner

Beth and Ivan Misner have been called international business tycoons by some, humanitarians by others, and by still others they are simply called Mom and Dad. All these names fit them quite well, and they have landed right in that sweet spot where life meets dreams and expectations.

Ivan is the founder of BNI and Beth is the cofounder of the BNI Foundation and creator of the Business Voices movement for children's education. Together they make an extraordinary couple.

BNI is Business Networking International and is the largest networking organization in the world.

But it wasn't always this way. Their story is one of patience, persistence, and extreme focus, which allows them to feel fully alive, pursuing their mutual passions.

Find Your Passion Through Patience and Persistence: Ivan and Beth Misner

(International Motivational Speakers, World Changers)

I was born in Pittsburgh, Pennsylvania, to a tall, lanky Korean War veteran and a diminutive and bubbly city girl. Relatively early in my life, the entire family—aunt, uncle, cousins, and grandparents—all moved to Los Angeles. Not just anywhere in Los Angeles, either. We moved to South Central Los Angeles.

My dad, Big Ivan as he was known, had not realized that he was moving his family into the 'hood. But we all learned quickly—especially me. As a six-year-old, I was an especially fast learner, as my mother loved to send me to school in sailor suits—hats and all. (Not exactly how to dress to blend in in South Central L.A.) I also learned I needed to develop some grit to steady myself against daily bullies.

Eventually, our family moved east and landed in Azusa, an unincorporated area of Los Angeles County, just in time to miss the Watts riots of 1965.

In the meantime, a young gal had come into the world in the great state of Texas. Elisabeth was a bright, eager-to-learn, outgoing girl. She loved to read, perform on the piano and sing, and she made friends easily. That much was good, since her dad specialized in construction engineering and moved from state to state following the work.

In 12 years of primary education, Beth attended eight different schools. One thing all her teachers and classmates remember about her is that she was a speed tester. She would get so hyper and revved up anytime a test of some sort was administered, that it seemed like a wormhole opened in the space-time continuum.

As individuals, we walked our separate paths, never knowing that our lives would intersect and we were being prepared perfectly for one another. When I was graduating from high school, my bride-to-be was just nine years old! (Now I am grateful that my Gen-X wife is around to share technology tips with me.)

As I grew, I recognized a stirring. I loved being a leader, and traits in this area began to emerge. During my student council classes in junior high and high school, I learned patience, persistence, and ways to be successful as a student leader. These strong qualities were juxtaposed with another side of me, one that was more aggressive.

One day my mom pulled me aside and said, "Son, if you don't develop a little diplomacy, you are never going to be elected to anything." She gave me a paperweight that had a saying etched into the top: ***Diplomacy is the art of letting someone else have your way.*** I tucked that saying away and let it begin to germinate.

The next year, I ran for student leadership . . . and came in dead last. Dead last! But that stayed with me and the little seed planted in my heart continued to sprout. The following year, I was asked by the homeroom teacher, Mr. Romero, if I would like to represent my class in student leadership. The rest of the class groaned. "Oh, no, not Ivan!" they began to wail.

Even though my classmates disagreed, I knew I could and would do a great job for the class. But I also knew I would have to have both the patience to win them over and the persistence to work on the issues that mattered to the student body. I set out to be the strongest freshmen class student body representative I could possibly be. By the time the year was over, I had enough support to be elected by my peers for sophomore student leadership.

It was then that I learned a little secret: I began to realize that the secret to success without hard work is still a secret! I knew I had to work hard to create credibility, and I knew I needed the support of other students in order to be able to continue in student leadership.

These truths followed me and engrained themselves in my life as a business leader. I always knew I would need to do the hard work necessary to gain credibility in business, just like I had to do in student leadership.

Through patience and persistence, I was elected again my junior year and then went on to become ASB (Associated Student Body) president my senior year. It was during these four years that I began to master the art of diplomacy. My experience in student leadership was so pivotal to my own future business success that I later formed the Misner Leadership Scholarship at my high school. The award is presented to the senior with the strongest record of student leadership.

Along the same lines, Beth, during her high school years, also developed the attributes of patience and persistence. Showing an aptitude for music at an early age, her piano teacher advised her parents to lead her to play the oboe in the junior high school band. Beth knew then that she wanted to go to college, but her parents also knew they had no money to send her to college. She would need to win one of the full-ride scholarships offered to excellent oboists who could play in their symphony orchestras.

Fortunately, she learned to play the oboe quickly, and soon reached a level of proficiency that allowed her to begin entering music contests. Each year she entered the local talent contest and placed higher in her division, working her way to that college scholarship. The first year she entered, she placed last. Bit by bit, she inched her way up to winning the district division for juniors (kids aged 12-14), and then began to win in the regional division for seniors (kids aged 15-17). Finally, she won tri-regionals one year and went to nationals, where she won first place and that college scholarship she needed.

That is where Beth's passion and persistence really started to pay off. Although she knew she was shooting for a full-ride scholarship, the practice hours required for the oboe were both intimidating and exhausting. Unlike the piano, which you can play for long periods of time without really getting tired, with the oboe, you can literally reach "failure," a point at which you can no longer keep the reed in your mouth at all. Her parents helped her, incentivizing her with time off to just be a kid once she reached a certain number of practice hours. She knew she had to do things she didn't want to do so she would be able to do the things she wanted to do.

It would have been easy for either of us to give up at the first experience of disappointment, deciding that reaching so high wasn't for us. We could have decided we were okay with simply being average or settling for something less than our dreams. But that wasn't part of our DNA. We both believed the old adage that we shouldn't settle for mediocrity when excellence was an option.

We were two people who were determined to follow our passions. But, of course, this couldn't happen overnight. We need those two things, patience and persistence, to make it happen.

It seems that for a very large part of their lives, most people can't even identify their passions. One day they find they are living someone else's life or working to further someone else's goals or dreams.

So when you truly recognize your passion, you have to summon the courage to chase it. We both very consciously made choices along the way that aligned with our greatest passions, and there is no greater joy than being in what I call the "flame." I believe that when you are working, you are either working in your "wax" (not your passion and strength) or you are working in your flame. If you only work in your wax, life will never be as fulfilling and rewarding as you hoped it would be.

But even digging deep to find your courage still might not be the final phase to living out your passion. For us, we still had more lessons to learn before we were able to begin working in our flame.

When we were married in 1989, Beth was 24, and I was 32. By this point, I was creating my touchstone, BNI, although it wasn't something I set out to do. I had lost my largest consulting client and was forced to create Business Networking International (BNI) out of necessity. At that time, I hadn't even had the vision or experience I needed to build a successful business network. I simply needed business referrals for my own consulting practice.

But before we knew it, BNI became the center of our professional lives as the company grew exponentially during our early years together. Beth traveled to undeveloped territories and helped the new BNI franchisees get their start, while I continued to create the corporate model and create the materials and marketing content, and wrote several books.

As an entrepreneur, I was interested in creating new businesses, so as people came to me with one new concept after another, I tried some of the new business ideas out.

This was where having extreme focus began to come into play. I tried one new idea after another, including these:

- Private Practice Network

- Salon Owners Guild

- Small Business Network

- Lunar Travel

- Business Funding Associates

I realized that the more splintered my focus became, the less effectively I was developing BNI to its full capacity. And bringing people together to create more success, more business, and more fulfillment, and helping them prosper was coalescing for me as my passion.

Writing and speaking helped to support these passions, and growing new businesses kept me from doing either of these things as often as I wanted to. I made a conscious choice to exercise extreme focus and stripped away everything that was not "vertically integrated"—that is, something that supported my primary passion. One of the vertically integrated projects we worked on together was creating the nonprofit arm of our company, the BNI Foundation.

I didn't realize it yet, but I had found my flame—my passion.

While I was exercising my creativity in the business world, Beth was spreading her wings and developing her talents and interests, too. Beth pursued several certifications, a black belt in karate, and a master's degree in theology, and started a Christian spiritual center, became a Tai Chi instructor, and wrote two books (both on different subjects, naturally), all while running the BNI Foundation and raising our three children. At one point she languished, "I don't know how to write a proper bio about myself. What is it that I really do? Am I a martial artist, a nutritionist, a theologian, a philanthropist? What?" Well, yes, yes, yes, and yes.

To help narrow her focus, I began to encourage her to do six things 1000 times, not 1000 things six times. "But I get bored if I try to narrow down the focus to just six things," she plaintively wailed. "How can you stand to just do six things? I need about 10 lives to do all the things I want to do and that I am interested in doing." It was definitely a quandary for her, and a frustration for me. Eventually she found the nerve to tell me my "six things 1000 times" refrain was actually kind of annoying to her. She wasn't sure that was a path she could enjoy.

But she could see at this point in our lives together that this formula was working well for me. I was becoming more and more fulfilled with my life, really hitting my passion stride by creating collaborative opportunities for others and inspiring them to make a difference through their own businesses—I was working in my flame. This stirred something within her, and the resistance to doing six things 1000 times lifted.

She came to understand that doing six things 1000 times doesn't mean all the interests she has must drop away completely. These interests have now appropriately been moved to the category of "hobbies" so she could focus on creating a movement we call Business Voices within the BNI Foundation. This movement uses all the talents and abilities she has to be a catalyst for systemic change in the arena of children's education.

Our business focus is now in lockstep with each other. We both are able to spend our days patiently, persistently exercising extreme focus to be as effective as we can, as we live life centered on our respective passions. As a result, we are traveling, speaking, and writing together—creating the life we dreamed we would have when we first embarked on our journey together as the Misners.

This life of following our passion certainly didn't happen overnight, but with patience and persistence, our passions are now at the forefront of our work together.

WHAT'S YOUR ACTION?

Meet Dale Brown

"The Master Motivator," Coach Dale Brown, not only has taken LSU basketball to new heights, he has been a champion for equality. With an admirable concern and consideration for others, he took on seemingly impossible challenges and beat the odds, time and time again as one of college basketball's finest coaches.

Coach Dale Brown, known for his "Freak Defense," has made an impressive number of consecutive NCAA appearances. Coach Brown had 17 consecutive winning seasons, and he's among just a handful of coaches who took teams to multiple Final Fours. In 1982, his College All-Star West team beat Coach Bob Knight's East team by 34 points.

He was honored as SEC Coach of the Year or Runner-Up nine different times and was selected twice for National Coach of the Year. His team beat Kentucky more than any other coach's team nationwide, a large percentage of his players completed their college education, and he was inducted in 2004 as an SEC Living Legend. Coach Dale Brown's time at LSU broke records for the largest audience of paying attendees in the history of college basketball. His determination and intense style have made him a top-notch inspirational speaker, and he was known as a critic of the NCAA because he felt their rules lacked compassion toward student-athletes.

After retirement, Coach Brown created Dale Brown Enterprises, worked as an analyst for college basketball, became the author of several books, and toured as a motivational speaker. The Dale Brown Foundation, which took a role in helping Louisiana hurricane victims, was established in 1986 as a way to help those in need. He took part on ABC's TV show *Shaq's Big Challenge*, helped motivate children who were overweight to become healthier, and worked with actor Matthew McConaughey, advising his role as football coach Jack Lengyel for the movie *We Are Marshall*.

Dale Brown is considered by many to be one of the greatest college basketball coaches in history.

Do Something: Dale Brown

(Coach, Author, Philanthropist,
and Master Motivator)

In 1806, the first dictionary ever written by Webster described success as being fortunate, happy, kind, and prosperous. This year, the Webster dictionary described success as: attainment of wealth, fame, rank, and power. When it comes to what we think success is, we have screwed up badly. We've lost our moral compass. We don't think we're successful unless we have wealth and power. As a result, we're bombarded with that kind of thinking every day.

And, yet, this has nothing to do with finding our passion.

I had no male role model, growing up. Two days before I was born, my so-called father abandoned my mother and my two older sisters. He never came back, never wrote, never sent us any money. We were left totally alone. My mother had been married right off the farm, and it was during the Depression, when times were especially tough on the cold plains of North Dakota. After my dad left, we moved into a one-room apartment with no bathroom, no toilet, no central heat or air (just radiators), no nothing. With only an eighth-grade education, my mother couldn't get a good job, so she cleaned people's homes, babysat, and had to go on welfare. She got $42.50 a month.

As a youth, I'd had a terrible inferiority complex. I felt self-conscious because our clothes smelled of mothballs, and we had no father. I didn't sleep in a bed for 21 years. No one in my family had been to college, so college was never mentioned. The one constant I had was my beautiful, fantastic mother. She never smoked, drank, never talked badly about anyone, and never once had anything negative to say. She had a bed that rolled out from the wall, and I had a sofa. She was about five feet, nine inches, and I was about six feet, three inches. I slept on the sofa like a question mark, but every night for 21 years, I could reach out and touch my mother's head. My life started differently than others'. It created a foundation of fearlessness.

Fearlessness started for me between the ages of 10 and 12. I remember being home, eating my soup. A welfare worker came to talk to my mother, who was such a spiritual, sensitive, lovely human being, but soft and easily hurt. My mother tried; she did everything she could. Our apartment was meticulous, but this lady was giving my mother all kinds of guff, and my mother was wringing her hands. I can still see the woman's black dress.

She told my mother, "I'll tell you one thing. Do you know that last month you spent 15 dollars on digitalis?"

I didn't know what that was but found out later it was a heart medication.

The woman said, "We give you $42.50 every month. What do you do with the money we give you?"

My mother replied, "We just barely make it."

The woman pointed over at me like I was a dog, didn't even say my name, not "son" or "boy" or "Dale," and said, "How about him? Can't he get a job?"

She told my mother to go get her purse so she could go through it. I remember eating that soup at 10 years old, sitting there saying to myself, "Never again. Never, as long as I live on this earth, will anyone ever intimidate a loved one of mine, or will I ever be intimidated."

I didn't know how to handle it at the time. I stayed quiet. I felt sorry for my mother, for the way she was humiliated. I knew I wanted to hit the woman who was bullying her.

Bullies are the biggest gutless wonders in the world, with their big mouths. The bully is the true phony.

Nobody burned that into me. I didn't have a dad; I had nothing, and I had an inferiority complex. No one ever came to our apartment. Paint peeled off the ceiling and fell down onto us. There were all sorts of smells and what have you. I only had two pairs of pants and two shirts, but they were meticulous. And I couldn't leave the house without my shoes shined. They had holes in the bottoms of them, but that didn't make any difference. It doesn't take a giant of a man to stand up.

Less than a month later, the final patchwork of this imperfect man was made. I came home again, and my mother was nervous, telling me, "Daley, you've gotta be careful. You can't go out into the hall and shoot baskets anymore."

I hadn't been able to afford a ball, so I'd folded socks up, taped them, and then shot them out into the hall. That's where I learned to shoot. The hall had linoleum, and my mother told me I couldn't go out into the hall to shoot baskets anymore because the landlady had come down to say, "That brat kid of yours is scuffing up my linoleum. Next time he does that, you'll be finding another place to live."

My mother told me I had to be careful.

I went out the door, sprung down the hallway, knocked on the landlady's door and when she opened it, said, "You leave my mother alone."

Then I walked down the hallway, scuffing her linoleum with my heels all the way. I guess that episode did it. I wasn't big; I was a little, skinny, insignificant, inferior kid. But the feeling just built, and then, just like that, I was able to spot injustices.

I didn't become a social worker, and I'm not a crusader, but right is right and wrong is wrong. Albert Einstein said that it isn't the bad people who are creating the problem, it's all of the good people who do nothing. Martin Luther King said it even more profoundly, asking why it was that the children of evil and darkness were so much more aggressive than the children of light and goodness.

My wife and I once visited Krakow, Poland, where the world-infamous incinerator concentration camp, Auschwitz, is located. The people there were gassed and burned. While we were going through it, I experienced all kinds of emotions. I felt like I wanted to punch one of the bad guys or use a machine gun on them. Then, I got depressed and melancholy. I finally said to my wife, "How in the hell . . . how could human beings do this to other human beings? I've gotta go outside."

It was a sunny, beautiful day, and I walked down a gravel road. I leaned up against a pole that I later found out was a railroad tie they'd used when gassing and incinerating people. I felt something on that tie. I looked up and found the answer to what had happened with it. On it were the words, "The road to Auschwitz was built by hatred, but was paved with indifference and apathy."

There it is. Apathy.

People don't speak up enough. We complain about those in Washington, D.C., but it seems I'm one of the only morons who's calling and writing to them about things. What have you done about it? A large majority of the people haven't done a doggone thing but complain. So, we get what we deserve: ineffective people in Washington. We simply don't know how to work together.

I was asked to run for U.S. Senate in North Dakota, and was told, "You're going to have to become more of a 'team player.'" The audacity! Immediately, I said, "Time out. You're telling me I have to be a 'team player'? Do you realize I've been coaching for 44 years? That was my theme! 'The best potential for me is we.' I know what the hell you're talking about, you're talking about partisan politics, and I'm not going to be a part of it. I told you from the start that I'm not a Republican or Democrat. I vote according to my heart, and the person. You've got the wrong guy."

The man replied, "I think you've misunderstood me."

No, no, no. So many times when you call someone out, they say you don't understand. No. That's exactly what they mean—jam that mitt. I didn't want to be a part of it.

Is all of Washington, D.C. that way? No. But not enough people are standing up and fighting. Too many are protecting their jobs. I've been in the service, and I'd give my life for this country. When I'd come back from other countries, I wanted to get down and kiss the tarmac, and say, "God bless America." I still do, but I would add an asterisk to that. God bless America, but wake up, America. We're going in the wrong direction.

I'm not a fatalist; some people call me more of a Pollyanna. But two and two is four, right is right, wrong is wrong. You can con yourself, say whatever you want, but we need to wake up from the coma. We've lost our moral compass—it's that simple. That's why we have the problems we have in the world.

People need to live out their passion. When I hear parents saying, "My son wants to be a doctor," I think, damn . . . seventh grade, and the kid knows he wants to be a doctor? Does he want to be a doctor, or is that the passion of his parents? Although there are too many parents who are not around, there are also some who live through their kids.

Too many people have delusions of grandeur. They try to be something they aren't and end up frustrated. That's not happiness. We talk about success, but seldom talk about happiness. I've seen some highly "successful" people; they've got it all, but they're unhappy as can be. So if being a doctor is what their kid wants to do, fine. But how would the kid know he wanted to be a doctor in seventh grade?

Thank God I got involved in athletics in seventh grade. And when I went to college, I went for one reason. To play ball. Football, basketball, and even track and field. I knew that if I didn't do well in high school sports, I didn't get a scholarship. I made sure I lettered in all of my sports.

As a senior, I met with the class counselor. At the time, I hadn't read much of anything and had never taken a book home. These days I'm a voracious reader who reads up to 100 books a year. But my counselor back then said, "What do you want to do?"

I said, "Eh, I want to be an FBI agent. Replace J. Edgar Hoover."

The counselor said, "—What? Dale Brown, do you realize where you're at? This is a state teacher's college. To become an FBI agent these days, you'll need a law degree, or some kind of degree."

I said, "Okay, then I'll teach and coach."

My friend Rick Pitino wrote a book, *Born to Coach*. I wasn't born to coach. I was just trying to make a living, help my mother get by. I chased balls or shoveled manure out of barns or drove taxis, just trying to survive. After my discussion with the counselor, one of my teachers turned on a switch—a history teacher, in fact. I hated history, but he made it vibrant and fun. From that time on, I was on a quest for learning.

After getting my first taste of coaching, I knew it was what I wanted. It was never a job to me—it was a passion. I loved what I did. I made up my mind, years ago while heading to LSU to coach, that when I didn't have the drive anymore, I'd retire. That's exactly what I did. I got up one day and didn't want to go to the office. The system had changed. I was sick of the recruiting. There were too many parasites and pimps hanging around. I went to speak to the Athletic Director and told him I'd be retiring.

I finished my coaching career and then sat back, looking over my 44 years, trying to decide where I was headed. While I was coaching, I really thought I did my very best, but once I retired, I recognized my limitations, my mistakes, and my distance from the ideal. Nothing could have stopped that from going on. After all, your "F.Q." (failure quotient) is far more important than your I.Q.

I went to another life, not really knowing what I wanted to do. We could've lived anywhere, done anything, but I went toward something I really love. I started working with Native Americans, trying to undo the injustices forced on them over the centuries. We are our brother's keeper.

Our roles as parents, coaches, and leaders are vital. Two times when I was a boy, in the middle of winter, I saw my frail little mother come home with brown paper shopping bags. She was so meticulous with her list, crossing out the peas, beans, potatoes, milk. Maybe once a month, she'd buy some meat. After arriving home, she'd put her big winter coat back on, and I'd ask, "Where are you going, Mama?"

She'd say, "The lady at the Red Owl gave me too much change. I've got to take it back to her."

I once saw her take a quarter back to the Piggly Wiggly. Do you think she had to teach me about ethics?

Actions are what we need.

St. Frances of Assisi in the 13th century told us we should preach the gospel every day, and if necessary, use words. Edward Guest said, "I'd rather see a lesson than hear one any day. I'd rather one would walk with me than merely tell the way. The eye's a better pupil, and more willing than the ear. And the lecture you deliver may be very wise and true, but I'd rather get my lesson by observing what you do."

Coach John Wooden was always so gracious. I'd known him for more than 40 years before he died. We were at a restaurant in Baton Rouge when an attractive-looking guy in a nice suit, about 45, approached. He said, "I don't want an autograph, I don't want to shake your hand, I don't want to take your picture. I just want to tell you something, sir. You are an angel of God. You're my hero. I idolize you. I just want you to know that."

Coach's reply was beautiful. He asked the man his name, and it was Derek. He said, "Derek, that's really kind of you, but I want you to know this about me. I'm not what I ought to be. I'm not what I could be. I'm not what I should be. But I'm sure glad I'm not what I used to be. You sure made me feel good today."

He always lowered the attention he was getting. I heard this story about him: After growing up in Martinsville, Indiana, he was getting ready to take off for Purdue University. His daddy walked him over to where he'd be catching a ride, put his arm around him and said, "Son, you're going off to the so-called big time right now. You can drive yourself crazy, but you won't. Johnny, never cease to be the best you can be because God doesn't make any junk, and that means you're more than enough."

Booker T. Washington was a slave, and his parents were slaves, yet he wound up consulting presidents and starting Tuskegee University. He said, "The role of most leaders is to get the people to think more of the leader. But the role of the exceptional leader is to get the people to think more of themselves."

That's a true leader.

If something isn't real, it won't last. If you're a phony, you're going to get caught. What you do will eventually be exposed into the light. The sad thing is that whenever evil and good come together and good compromises, evil always wins.

Let's talk about the difference one person can make. Telamachus was a monk living in a cloistered monastery outside of Rome during the fifth century. He'd never been to Rome, but once he got caught up in the people and traffic and wound up at the top tier of the Roman Colosseum. There he saw gladiators slashing each other. When one was beheaded, the monk was stunned, speechless. He wondered if it was all fake, a show, and waited for the man to get back up. But he didn't.

Then, the same thing happened again. Telemachus stood up on the back row in his cloistered outfit, put his hands into the air and loudly said, "Please, please. In the name of God, somebody stop this!"

The people were half-drunk and probably threw grapes at him. Another battle was getting ready to start. Telemachus ran down to the retaining wall and shouted, "Please, please, in the name of God, stop this!"

The men pulled out their swords. Telemachus ran out into the middle of the Colosseum and got onto his knees before the two men, pleading, "Please, please, in the name of God, stop this killing and murder. Stop it now!"

The king gave the sign to get rid of him. They didn't behead him—they slashed open his bowels. Telemachus fell face down, bleeding, and died there on the sandy Colosseum floor. A silence came over the stadium. This man that no one knew had just perished before them. Suddenly, the people started to exit the stadium, leaving the stands only half-filled.

Fifteen days later, the king of Rome signed a decree ending all gladiator matches. From that day on, no more matches were fought in that Colosseum, all because of that one man, Telemachus.

Everyone else just sits there, complaining, but are they doing anything about it? Are you going to do something about any of the injustices you see?

I mentioned I didn't have a dad growing up. Once, at the school I went to, I got kicked out of class for swearing at a tough old missile of a nun. She went and got the coach, who said to me, "What did you call her?"

I said I swore at her. He said, "Is that what you said, you swore at the sister? What did you say?"

I told him I'd called her a son of a bitch.

He grabbed my shirt, twisted it, and bumped my head against the locker. He didn't mean to hit me, but his knuckle cut my lip. I had my fist folded, and thought, "All these worthless men. As soon as he lets go, I'm gonna drive him right across the hallway."

He then grabbed me on the back of the neck and said, "Get back in there, man. I love you, Dale Brown."

Then, he took off. I watched him walking down the hall and with my lip cut and my shirt all screwed up, I thought, "As a senior in high school, that's the first man who ever told me he loved me."

The result was that when he went to my basketball games, he'd stand by the water fountain, and I'd dunk. I increased in elevation, just because one man told me he loved me.

I was talking to John Wooden once in his modest condominium. He wouldn't turn the air conditioning on, and it was hotter than heck in there. I said, "Coach, your life is so simple, not complicated." He said, "Dale, the thing we should all learn is this: The three most important things in life are happiness, freedom, and peace. You cannot have any of them unless you are giving them to someone else."

Don't want to get involved? Just remember Auschwitz. It's what happens if you don't get involved. That road is paved with hatred but built by indifference. I once spoke to 5,000 Naval Academy cadets about moral courage. Maya Angelou's description was perfect: "Courage is the most important of all virtues, because without courage, you can't practice any other virtue consistently."

You don't have to be a world scholar to figure it out. Instead of asking ourselves how we can beat the system and begrudgingly accept change, *we* can change. Every major revolution from the beginning of time involved only 12 or fewer men—every major one. It didn't take a battalion or regiment; it just took a few people being creative.

What if you don't think you're good enough to serve in that way? Oscar Wilde said, "Every saint has a past, and every sinner has a future."

When my wife and I visited the mountains of the Czech Republic, we stayed with a pleasant, older couple for several days. One night, we'd just had dinner and were walking back to our little pensione when Bonnie said, "You know what, Dale? I'm convinced that the most extraordinary people on this Earth are the most ordinary people."

We put our movie stars and athletes on pedestals. There are so many more famous people that the population doesn't even know about. But God knows about them, and that's the most important thing. They are the people who stand up for injustice and refuse to be silent.

WHAT'S YOUR ACTION?

_____

_____

_____

_____

_____

_____

_____

_____

_____

_____

_____

_____

_____

_____

_____

_____

_____

_____

Meet Jamie Anderson

Jamie Anderson grew up in South Lake Tahoe, California, as the fifth of eight children. At age 15, she won a bronze medal at the 2005 Winter Games for snowboarding, making her the youngest competing female medalist. She also won gold medals at the Winter Games in 2007/2008, and 2012/2013, and the gold medal for the inaugural women's slope style event at the 2014 Sochi Winter Olympics as well as in the 2018 PyeongChang Winter Olympics.

She's known to be one of the top slope-style riders in the world.

While others are still dreaming about reaching their passion, Jamie Anderson is making it happen.

Recognize Your Intrinsic Passion: Jamie Anderson

(Professional Snow Boarder and Olympic Gold Medalist/Sochi and PyeongChang Olympics)

My parents chose to homeschool my brothers, my sisters, and me. We were raised in the mountains where we had the freedom to grow, learn, and explore nature, finessing the opportunity to really find passion for our interests. I feel unbelievably grateful for the way I grew up. We are a family filled with people who love to snowboard.

Being outside was my favorite thing. Camping, hiking, skiing. It didn't matter. I loved it all. Being in the snow was my favorite. When I was really young, we sledded, built crazy toboggan hills, and hiked the mountains. When I was nine, my two older sisters had already been into snowboarding for a couple of years, and I finally got hand-me-down equipment from them. I joined the Sierra Team, and Sierra Tahoe became my first sponsor. Once I got into it, it was the easiest thing in the world to do because I was in love with it. Since we were homeschooled, my sisters and I were able to be on the mountain almost every day—exploring, riding, and eating a packed lunch together.

Snowboarding is a soul sport. Connecting with nature, being in the mountains, exploring new terrain. It's always creative and inspiring to go to the different parks, and it's a challenge. You get there and it's intimidating, difficult to figure out. By the end of the week, you're able to hit it and do your tricks, things you didn't even think were possible. That passion keeps me going.

Finding that love and passion at such a young age was the start of my journey. I began competing in all the events, but learned that I enjoyed foot style most. At 13, my coach decided I should attend a local X Games qualifier in Tahoe. It was one of the craziest competitions; I'll always remember it. My older sister Joanie had already qualified, so we experienced it together for the first time. I was a tiny girl competing against 20-year-olds but ended up winning the event. My passion was already bringing me so much joy.

At 15, I qualified for slope style. It was so creative and different that I was thrilled to pour energy into it. That year I won a bronze medal at the Winter Games, the U.S. Open, and the Vans Cup. That's when it really happened. I started winning some professional events and signed with Billabong, my first sponsor.

Because I grew up in a big family and this is such an expensive sport, I was blessed that companies like Billabong provided me with everything I could need. I was inspired to work hard to get what I wanted. My mom taught me how to work hard, whether that meant selling golf balls from the river or helping with her lawn care business. No job was too little or too big.

When I was 17 and my sister was 21, we both won our first gold medals at the X Games. It was the first year my whole family came out. She was competing, I was competing. I won and she won, and it was surreal and unbelievable.

I'd never thought about being in the Olympics. Qualifying for Sochi came out of nowhere; suddenly everything connected. I always thought going to the Olympics was an amazing opportunity, but I wasn't passionate about half pipe. I even attempted to go to the Vancouver Olympics for half pipe but didn't give it all my love. I hadn't ridden the pipe enough, didn't have the drive to do it, and didn't qualify for the team. I was okay with that. I was loving what I was doing, having a great time, and I had no regrets. I knew the half pipe wasn't my passion.

Then the Olympic committee announced the slope-style event would be added to the Olympics. This changed everything—I'd been at ease with not going for half pipe before and hadn't made a big deal of it. But when they announced they were adding my event, I felt like the universe was on my side. I'd been doing really well at it. I had the support and the ability to travel the world and a freedom I hadn't ever known.

I was about 22 and remember being so excited, but also thinking I didn't want to change my life. If I did, things could turn crazy in a split second. I hadn't had a coach since I was 14 or so. I'd just been doing my own thing. If I chose not to try for the Olympics, I could continue —I'd been having fun and progressing in my riding, but not anything that would take me out of my comfort zone.

I tried not to get wrapped up in what other people were saying or posting online. If they thought I was the best, the favorite to win the Olympics, that put a lot of pressure on me. It was in my nature to be respectful, to thank them, but I tried not to guarantee anything. I just focused on doing my best, having no attachment to the outcome. I would be doing it all for a higher reason, not for the purpose of being the best or padding my ego. I tried to stay humble and grateful. This wasn't for myself, it was part of my path. Yet I also had to accept it if my path wasn't to win.

Going into it, interviewers and many of those who were talking to me said I would win. For me, it took a lot of mental and psychological work to really hold it together. I practiced a lot of yoga, meditation, and affirmations, really believing it. Before the win happened, I knew, intrinsically, that I was going to win.

It's scary to set big goals and know that you might not reach them. That's a possibility. I knew it was going to be a part of my journey, but I didn't tell people, "Yeah, I'm going to win." But in my own practice, I really did have to believe it was going to happen, and manifest it and write about it, read about it, and stay on my right path. I connected my passion to my mind, body, and spirit.

That was my goal that winter and throughout the chaos. I was so grateful to be able to stay true to myself, to focus, achieve, and do what I was meant to do. It was beyond gratifying.

To stay grounded, I relied on my family and those around me. My mom in particular gave me continual encouragement to follow through, to maintain my integrity, and to be the best person I could possibly be. She taught me to work hard and live in the moment, always being present and passionate about the path I am on.

It's all what you make of any situation. When I am living my passion, there is no reason not to enjoy every second.

WHAT'S YOUR ACTION?

_____

_____

_____

_____

_____

_____

_____

_____

_____

_____

_____

_____

_____

_____

_____

_____

_____

_____

_____

Meet Ryan Smith

I had the privilege of meeting Ryan during a Power Up weekend seminar that he and his company were holding. In an instant, you could tell this guy had it all. He was good looking, tall, smart, successful, and had a way with the spoken word.

He used words to their fullest capacity—a wordsmith, really—but he made even the most complex topics easy to understand.

Ryan has more than 15 years of extensive business experience and is considered an expert in market evaluation, property analysis, management systems, due diligence, finance, and more.

He graduated from the University of Tampa with a Bachelor of Science in Computer Science. An athlete, Ryan was highly recruited for both baseball and basketball and was drafted as a senior in high school by the Baltimore Orioles. He pursued his athletic talents by playing baseball throughout his college experience.

His foresight and ability to communicate the state of the marketplace has propelled him to be a featured commentator alongside the likes of Rudy Giuliani, Ben Stein, General Colin Powell, and many more.

He is one of the most humble people I have met, and one of the most successful.

Believe in Yourself: Ryan Smith

(Financial and Business Expert, Entrepreneur, Real Estate Giant)

I meet a lot of retirees who think our country's "going to hell in a handbasket." They think our young people don't have any manners, and when I hear that, I want to say, "Well, who raised them? Who did they learn that from?"

It doesn't matter who you care about, how jaded you are, or what impression you want to make. If I dig deep enough in the garden of your mind, there's a part of you that wants to make a meaningful impact. Through business, you can actually do that.

I love this concept of "meaningful capitalism." I've been encouraged by the fact that you can teach people, specifically young people, that capitalism is a pursuit of excellence, a humbling of yourself, an efficiency to arrive at economic profit. Through your pursuits, the economic return yields a social return in terms of your charity. A lot of young people think it's cool to be able to take their skills, make money, serve people, give to those they care about, and have a good life. They say, "That's great. Where do I sign up?"

The problem isn't that the kids are spoiled rotten, or that they don't want to help. The problem is this: Who is teaching them? Although there are many reasons for concern about our country, there are also a lot of reasons to have hope. There is fertile ground within the minds of our young people. Many of those in the generation before us weren't willing to plant the seeds, all the while yelling about how there isn't much of a harvest. That doesn't solve the problem.

I owe a lot to my grandfather. I consider him the smartest man I ever met. He made some big investments at a young age and then helped all of his grandkids gain financial literacy. Each year, he carefully selected stock to purchase, and bought $1,000 worth of stock for each of us. He'd share with us why he bought stock in that particular company. As a second grader, I'd pick up the newspaper to see how the companies' stock was doing that day and see how they'd done the day before. If I was riding to school with friends and they started drinking a Pepsi, I'd get on them. I had ownership in Coke. Coke was superior, and how dare they? I wanted them to buy my product.

I was a young entrepreneur, an advocate for capitalism. I became passionate about innovation—finding better ways to do things. I loved trying to make things more efficient, loved simplifying complex processes. By age nine, I began getting paid to program. By age 13, companies paid me to hack into their computer systems and then tell them how I got in, so they could plug the holes in their security.

At 13, I also started a company dealing with a local Orlando manufacturer of tea light candles, which were made for Nordstrom, Neiman Marcus, and other high-end retailers. They were a wholesaler; they had no retail. The buddy I partnered with was 30 years old and had some technological expertise. The value I brought was programming the websites to have shopping carts and merchant accounts. This was before the time of API interface accounts and shopping carts. I had access to the whole thing and became the retail end for the wholesaler. Although my partner wasn't necessarily sophisticated in business, I learned a lot. But that first real enterprise failed because it was a terrible idea, and it didn't work.

I got that out of my system at 13, and it was a great experience for me. When you're young, no one expects you to succeed, so you're not going to be letting anyone down. The worst that could happen is that you fail, and if you do, you'll be meeting expectations. But if you win, you've just proved them all wrong.

In baseball, they call that a "free swing." Bases loaded, full count, and the pitcher's going to underhand the ball right down the plate, but he's going to tell you before he does. Swing for the fence.

Young people have a free swing to hit a home run; they just have to see it that way. Adults do, too, but a lot of times you'll meet people who are 30, 40, or 50 years old who complain about how no one believes in them. Not their parents, not anyone. That's great! No one's putting any expectations on you, so how free are you? You can't lose.

The real problem occurs when a person places no expectations on *themselves*. That's really what they're complaining about.

The next company I went into had to do with consulting for technology. It was the early '90s, before Amazon or online shopping was popular. I had an online store and a lot of expertise in something people were just starting to get curious about. I began to do a lot of consulting work, since businesses paid a lot of money to help build out their shopping carts.

The problem with that company was that I only got paid for my time, and I learned as a teenager that I did not like getting paid in direct correlation to my time. I made good money but didn't like the relationship.

The third company involved my dad, who was a decent real estate investor. My dad invested by gut, not mathematics. Since financial forecasting wasn't his forte, he used to have me go into his office and pull up Excel spreadsheets, forecasting for his real estate deals. At 14 years of age, I was responsible for capitalization rates, cash-on-cash returns, and internal financial returns.

After working with about 100 deals on properties, I decided to create a tool that would do the financial forecasting. Sixty codes later, I had a program that even he could use. It didn't originate for commercial reasons; I created it to help my dad. After showing it to a few people, other investors began saying, "Wow, that's really great! Could it do this? Could it do that?" I said, "It sure can."

I started calling some other wholesalers who might have interest in my software. I called different distribution channels, telling them, "If I had a program that did x, y, and z, would you be interested?"

They'd ask, "When can I take a look?"

I'd think to myself, how long would it take me to program a, b, and c? I'd set a date in my mind, write the software, and add the features they'd requested, knowing that if I did, I'd already have a buyer. I got enough distributors and channels, and sold 150,000 copies of the software. During my sophomore year at college, my revenue was around $800,000, all profit. That third technology company, dealing with real estate investment and decision analysis software, was a great business. With that, I made a couple of million dollars by college graduation.

From that business I learned to take something that is seemingly complex and make it easy—and usable.

When it came to sports, I was always an athlete. I was a six-foot, eight-inch basketball player in high school, and I was great at it because I worked my tail off. I was one of those gym rats who practiced between three and four hours daily. I loved the sport.

By the time I was a senior, I had letters for basketball from a lot of mid-level D1 and D2 schools like Lake Forest, Duke, North Carolina, and some others. I knew I was good at basketball from sheer work ethic, but I was short on talent, even though I had the height and other things that were a benefit to me. From a baseball standpoint, though, I had a natural gift to throw hard at 94 miles per hour, without working at it at all.

I went to a specific high school because it was one that endorsed two-sport athletes. As a senior, I was among the top 100 United States basketball players and among the top 30

United States pitchers. The coach who supported me in playing basketball retired at the end of my junior year and was replaced by another coach who had a very different policy. Not only did he dislike two-sport athletes, he punished athletes who didn't focus on one sport. I was already established at that school, so I tried to work it out and just survive my senior year.

That senior year, we went to the state finals or regionals in basketball. Because we excelled in basketball and with the way the season works, I missed the first two weeks of baseball season. By that time, I was one of the top 30 prospects in the United States for pitching. All of the teams were trying to recruit me, since throwing 94 miles per hour was an attractive prospect for most major leagues.

When I was supposed to pitch my first game of the year, there were about 30 scouts in the stands from every team you could imagine. They were there because we all thought I was going to be the starting pitcher. When the coach saw the scouts in the stands, he started someone else and benched me—my punishment for playing basketball. I hoped that would be a one-time occurrence, but it went on throughout the entire season. Any game the scouts attended, he'd bench me and not allow me to pitch.

I tried to address this. With my parents, we went to the principal, and we went to the local school board. I have no idea what the issue was with the coach. At the time I was the head of FCA, the Fellowship of Christian Athletes. We had a huge FCA at our school. People knew what I was and what I stood for.

At the games where the scouts were, I eventually asked my girlfriend, who sat in the stands, to go get the scouts and show them to the bullpen, where I'd asked my friend Alan to catch for me. When the scouts gathered, I said, "Guys, I'd love to pitch for you today, but for whatever reason, whenever you show up, the coach won't let me pitch. So I'm going to throw bullpen for you right here, and you can decide whether or not I'd be of interest to you."

I got drafted on the bullpen.

I only pitched eight innings my entire senior year. Our team had some great people and good players, but we needed good pitching. We had a terrible season.

While being considered for the draft, there were several months that passed before they drafted on the curve, so I visited Mississippi State, Auburn, and Georgia Tech for baseball. I finally accepted a baseball scholarship to the University of Georgia.

It had actually been my dream to play there. The grandfather I loved and adored was an alumnus, and lived in Athens, Georgia, right near the university. I was thinking I'd get to spend time with him, going to school so close. My mom was a big Georgia Bulldog and had at one time dated Coach Ray Goff, back when they were in college. There was a family history there, and I was set on Georgia.

After pulling the stunt of promoting myself and getting the interest of the scouts during high school baseball season, the coach called the University of Georgia and told him I was an out-of-line, disrespectful kid. The University of Georgia revoked my scholarship.

That was tough.

Since I'd already told Mississippi State, Auburn, and Georgia Tech I'd chosen the University of Georgia, they'd already filled my spot. In addition, Ben Knapp and I were two local prospects the Baltimore Orioles were interested in. Ben was a good six-foot, six-inch pitcher, and threw at about 91 miles per hour. I had more velocity and was probably more upside, but because I'd only pitched eight innings my senior year and Ben had pitched 50, the Orioles took him in the third round, and not me.

I fell to the eighth round. The guy who drafted me later told me he wanted me in the third round, but I'd been put in a bad light by one man, so there was a lot of adversity. I found myself graduating and not wanting to sign professionally because of that eighth round. There was a nice bonus, but I already had a business, so the money wasn't overly compelling to me, although I did still want my education. So, I got on the phone and found the best junior college in the country, called the coach, told him all about myself and my situation, and then said I'd like to come and throw the ball for him.

When I tried out, I threw two balls, and the coach said, "You have a full ride."

I played for the first year, thinking I wouldn't be staying at junior college. I was just trying to work my way back, but when I pitched a game during my second year, I pitched six innings and struck out 17 people. With six innings and 18 batters, that's the best you can do. They were one of the top teams in the country, and during that game I threw 96 miles per hour.

There happened to be a scout for the Angels in the stands named Tom Kotchman. He'd been in town and heard about the game. After watching me and talking to me, and even though I told him I wanted to get my education and go to school, he drafted me anyway. Since he was from Oregon, I went to Oregon State so he could watch me play.

What my high school coach put me through was a great process through which I matured. Absolutely fantastic. If I could go back and change the circumstances, I wouldn't. I don't harbor any ill feelings. At the time I did, for sure. At the time I didn't think much of him, but at this point, I wouldn't change it if I could. The net results from that experience will last throughout my career.

As I progressed at college, I grew my technology and software business. I made $800,000 my sophomore year, and another $600,000 the next year. I remember going to practice and watching my coach, whose salary I'd looked up, and thinking, here's this great guy that I respect. He works his tail off and makes one-eighth of what I made this year. He's at the top of his game, coaching one of the top teams in the U.S., and he's making an eighth.

Of course, I didn't tell anybody how much I made. It was hard, being a college kid who was excited about what I was doing, but I couldn't tell anyone. If I did, they wouldn't believe me—or if they did believe me, they'd want to take advantage of me. There was a whole list of negative ramifications that could come from sharing that joy.

By my senior year of college, after doing some tryouts, the Atlanta Braves approached me and were interested in signing. That was when I chose between baseball and business. I really did enjoy baseball, but ultimately knew I had a talent for business. I was more passionate about the new frontiers of innovation, efficiency, and automation. I was really developing myself, expanding my own horizons.

The other factor was that in baseball, someone owns you. I couldn't get past the concept of someone owning me and telling me, here's a check, go here, do that. I didn't like that, and I didn't like the business of baseball.

I was much better off with the type of business I could control, one where I had realized my potential. Rather than join someone else's business, I remained in business for myself. It was a good decision, and I was fortunate to have been able to make it. Many of those I went to school with went on to play baseball, at least minor league. They didn't think they had options. It always comes down to what you think and how you choose to pursue your passions.

Everyone on the face of the planet has a lot to contribute. The question to ask is this: What is the purpose behind what you do each day? Is it to get something, or to give something?

If your only goal is to get, you won't get much. The beauty of giving is that it's like a boomerang. What you throw out there, you get back. If your sole purpose is to give, you both give and get—that's the way it works. If your focus is on giving and making a meaningful impact on those you care about and in the marketplace, church, community, charities, and your family, there's never a day when you say, "not today."

You won't find yourself saying you don't care about helping your family, or that your church can go pound sand. You'll be excited and you'll hope the day yields fruit because that fruit will help others. That's what you'll be passionate about.

One of the biggest mistakes people make is to set goal posts. They say, "Here's where I am, here's where I'm going, here's where I want to be," and they miss the point. They weren't looking beyond that—they were looking to get a pre-defined result and missed the big opportunity.

In the story of the Good Samaritan, people were passing by the injured man. The story stated who they were and where they were going. They had destinations and were probably behind schedule and didn't want to be inconvenienced. The Good Samaritan didn't have anywhere he had to be; he was on a journey that didn't have an end. Because of that, he was able to spend time helping another person, and he got a cool, unexpected result.

One of the guys I've had the privilege of learning from, who is second only to my grandfather as the most influential person in my life, made such an amazingly simple statement. For someone who's not really listening, it wouldn't sound magical. But if you are searching for a way to get where you want to go, it's all rooted in what he said:

"Believe in yourself."

If you want to be successful, you have to believe in yourself. I believe action is rooted in belief. If you don't believe, you won't take a step forward because no one has enough faith for that.

If you believe in yourself, you'll take the step. It starts with a belief that it is possible—if you have an idea or inkling of how you can better the lives of other people and ultimately better your life, your church, your community.

As a result of that belief, you take action and realize the potential of your belief. But if you don't have that belief, you'll never take action and ultimately, all those you care about will not benefit. It's circular. For me, it's the opportunity to serve, to be a blessing, to help people's light bulbs come on so you can help everybody in the process. This is the passion that leads me.

You don't take a step out in faith. You take a step out in belief.

WHAT'S YOUR ACTION?

From Stories to P.A.S.S.I.O.N.

If you have a goal, if you have passion, if you are persistent and put that passion into action, you'll surprise yourself by your own drive. You will not only make it, you will far surpass your initial goals.

You must understand, realize, and *know this:* the only person who can get in the way or has the power to stop you from succeeding is yourself. Likewise, nobody else is going to do the work for you. It must be something you want, desire, and are willing to work for.

The following pages give you the foundational steps toward putting your passion into action.

This course is available to anyone at
www.mypassioninaction.com

Passion

The more passionate you are about yourself, your work, your life, or whatever it is that you do every day, the more positive and fulfilled you will be. Finding a way to be content isn't always easy, but the road is far less turbulent if you are living passionately. Sincere happiness, joy, and freedom come when you are doing something you love. You cannot buy passion off a shelf. It comes from within, and it's common for most to not know what their own passion is.

Some may use terms such as, "my calling," "my purpose," or "what I long for," but regardless of the phrase or word, "it" shapes our existence and adds fuel to the fire of inspiration, motivation, and success.

Together, we will explore in detail your personality, gifts, talents, strengths, areas for growth, and the great possibilities you can make happen, rather than wishing and hoping something will just magically take place.

Passion happens when you are authentic, do what you love, and know deep in your soul it's what you should be doing. When your actions are in alignment with your passion, many great things happen, both personally and profession-ally. Instead of watching the clock, hoping for time to pass by quickly, you will find yourself wishing there were more hours in a day because you love what you are doing.

Living with intention and by design, rather than by de-fault or waiting for something to happen, can make your entire world change. If you aren't living with passion, you are simply existing—going through life numb, waiting, wishing, and hoping. I want to help you stop just existing and make incredible changes that will be—without trying to sound dramatic—life changing. Your dreams, goals, desires, and PASSION are waiting for you. The question really is, "Are you ready?"

The program's first module helps identify your strengths with two in-depth, detailed, and scientific assessments. These assessments identify what makes you tick and how you re-spond to things, and allows you to formulate a course of action. This is a crucial and important step that will start your journey on the right path.

Action

Many people have fantastic ideas, goals, or inventions that nobody will hear about. Likewise, countless people will never reach the goals they set for themselves. It's far easier to think or talk about something than take action and do the required work to make it a reality.

In many cases, the lack of (or complete absence of) action isn't necessarily due to laziness, but something more obvious. It's human nature to come up with goals, ideas, and big dreams, but the reason most people aren't successful in accomplishing them is simple: they don't know where to start.

Learning how to grow and reach or exceed the goals you set for yourself is critical, both personally and professionally. Setting goals and taking steps toward them, with accountability and tracking methods, brings the accomplishment, success, and outcome you desire. Yes, it takes work—sometimes very hard work—so you must be steadfast in carving out the life you desire.

With that said, you have likely heard of, tried, or downloaded some tool to help you with setting goals, maybe more than once. I have tried many programs, spreadsheets, paper, digital, and apps (applications), and the list goes on and on. Unfortunately, I found accountability, measurement, and an action plan within my goal set to be missing.

This led me to the development of My Daily Guide©, which if done correctly, will increase the likelihood that you will reach your goals by more than 74 percent.

My Daily Guide© is an extremely useful and successful tool to reach your goals and clearly define and manage your time. Now, I must say that time management is a misnomer, as nobody on the planet can honestly manage time. Time is an invisible measurement, so instead of trying to manage an intangible object, there is a more successful way: managing your priorities.

The second module of the program is centered around taking action and moving forward. Using my system, you will learn how to determine what goals to set based on where you are and how you want to reach these goals. On top of that, you will learn how to manage your priorities effectively with the use of My Daily Guide©.

Self

It is my personal belief that everything starts internally, in your mind and heart. If you desire to be a high-end CEO or the best stay-at-home parent you can be, it all starts from within.

Decades ago, if you focused on yourself you might be considered stuck-up, self-absorbed, or conceited. In today's' society, it seems as though everything is about focusing on yourself and inward thinking. Instant this, instant that, instant gratification, make yourself better in mind, body, and spirit, the whole shebang. In fact, the "Self-Help" industry sells a whopping 11 billion dollars per year, and yet so many people are not happy and are suffering. Why?

I believe it's due to an imbalance of tools and resources that actually work and make a difference, compared to the motivational hype, the "you can do anything" attitude. Also, what people are told to focus on isn't going to sustain them long term. People who buy books, programs, or go to big-name seminars and retreats are highly pumped up and ready to take on the world shortly after they leave. The problem, and sad reality, is that after a few days "life" gets in the way and they fall back into the same routines, making no forward progress.

I am not suggesting you can't obtain value from seminars, but I want you to answer these questions. How many self-help books, programs, or seminars have you attended in the last five to ten years? Do you know where all the materials they gave you, or the books you read, are located? Have you ever come home after one of these seminars or after reading a book, felt motivated, and then put them back on the shelf—to be rarely, if ever, looked at again?

My program will motivate you, not through smooth-talking smoke and mirrors, but rather by implementing tools and resources that work, and most importantly, are sustainable.

The third module of my program is centered around you. You will learn about self-confidence, self-worth, and your value to the world. You will take assessments, learn about calendar blocking and how to invest in yourself in a healthy manner, learn your gifts and strengths, define success, and so much more. After you position yourself in a great spot, you can serve others, which leads us to the next module.

Service of Others

Helping or serving others is not usually (if ever) a topic you come across in a program like this. However, serving others is one of the most critical things you can do to help yourself grow and develop. That sounds backwards, doesn't it? Let me explain.

Scientifically, studies have shown that helping others can add years to your life. Part of the reason is that volunteering, helping, or serving others eliminates loneliness and increases your social life, oftentimes expanding your circle of friends and influence.

Studies have also proven that serving others can reduce blood pressure and chronic pain, and it is contagious—it causes a ripple effect. When you serve others, you are not only helping them, but you are teaching those around you and leading by example.

Think about the last time you donated your time in the service of others. How did it make you feel? I'm guessing it made you feel good, but what actually takes place inside is a neurochemical sense of reward. This is why we all love giving a gift equally, and often more than receiving one. Sociologists studied 2,000 people, and those who described their life to be "very happy" averaged almost six hours of volunteerism per month.

Please don't confuse the service of others with just another task you have to do, or that you are going to be required to spend your own money. In fact, as you go through this module, you will find that it becomes not only a habit, but it's something that you can't live without. Would you believe that most people who are truly in need would choose a small amount of your time over your money?

An old Chinese proverb tells it perfectly: "If you want happiness for an hour, take a nap. If you want happiness for a day, go fishing. If you want happiness for a year, inherit a fortune. If you want happiness for a lifetime, help somebody."

The fourth module of my program discusses how serving others will benefit you, and all the rewards that come with it. We will discuss why it's critical, what happens when you sincerely invest in others (not financially), and also where to start. There will also be weekly and monthly challenges to consider undertaking.

Investment & Inventory

When you hear the words investment and inventory, what comes to your mind? If you are like many people, visions of financial portfolios and money pop right up.

When you think of the word investment, perhaps ideas of buying land, a home to rent, or purchasing stocks come to mind. The goal of an investment, in short, is to purchase something expecting it will yield more value in the future than you paid, creating a profit.

Yet, how often do you invest in yourself? Have you ever done it at all? Investing in yourself is one of the most powerful ways to increase your joy, happiness, and contentment, yet it's rare for most people to do. What have you invested in for yourself that will yield far greater profit than money? Additionally, what relationships do you invest in—or more importantly, what relationships are you *not* investing in?

When you think of the word inventory, most people envision a large retail company counting all of their merchandise and then comparing it with their computer reports. If you have less than you thought you had, it's considered a loss. Likewise, if you have more, it's called an overage.

How many things on your life's "shelf" are just taking up space and not yielding you anything positive? Is your self-inventory valuable and sustainable, or is it dragging you down? Do you have any idea what your full self-inventory contains?

When you think about what you have invested in yourself and your relationships, and you begin taking a personal inventory, it can seem overwhelming and unclear what that even means—let alone how to start. When done correctly, it can be an eye-opening experience and one that increases your profit (life).

The fifth module of my program walks you through a step-by-step process that provides a clear picture of your personal inventory, showing you how to identify and remove things that aren't needed. The module also provides ways to invest in yourself and others so that you can receive dividends for the rest of your life.

Obstacles

How do you react when an issue shows up in your life? Life's obstacles are not supposed to paralyze you, but instead they can provide opportunities to discover who you really are. We've all heard what doesn't kill us makes us stronger, right? Well, I'd prefer to have solutions in place to help me minimize and break through these issues, wouldn't you?

I contend that handling an issue or obstacle in the best way possible is much easier said than done. There are so many theories, suggestions, and methods on how to handle obstacles that the solutions themselves are overwhelming and too plentiful.

Wouldn't it be nice to have a game plan when you encounter a difficult situation, or a how-to set of instructions for overcoming an obstacle? We provide a relatively simple approach that helps break obstacles down so they aren't so daunting, and it has been proven to be quite effective.

We all have different kinds of obstacles at varied times in our lives and some are harder than others, understandably. Although there isn't a one-size-fits-all approach to every obstacle, there are proven ways to help solve and diffuse them that can enable you to handle them.

My mother passed away five years ago, which as you can imagine, was devastating. If someone told me to take a module to "fix" this obstacle (my feelings of grief and loss), I would have quickly dismissed it, shortly after telling them they were crazy. Although the tools we provide have been proven successful, if you feel you have an obstacle that seems monumentally overwhelming, such as a death in the family, I don't contend that it should replace therapy or seeing a professional.

It's crucial to have a foundational approach for what to do when obstacles present themselves—that is why this module is so important. You can turn a negative into a positive and learn perspective when analyzing obstacles.

The sixth module is very important and close to my heart. We all have issues and obstacles in life and sadly, we always will. After completing this module, you should feel more comfortable and confident in overcoming obstacles or difficult situations in a more efficient, timely, positive, and healthy manner. We provide tools and resources that allow you to assess, work through, and successfully overcome challenges.

Nurture the New You

The more passionate you are about yourself, your work, your life, or whatever it is that you do every day, the more positive and fulfilled you will be. Finding a way to be content isn't always easy, but the road is far less turbulent if you are living passionately. Sincere happiness, joy, and freedom come when you are doing something you love. You cannot buy passion off a shelf. It comes from within, and it's common for most to not know what their own passion is.

Some may use terms such as, "my calling," "my purpose," or "what I long for," but regardless of the phrase or word, "it" shapes our existence and adds fuel to the fire of inspiration, motivation, and success.

Together, we will explore in detail your personality, gifts, talents, strengths, areas for growth, and the great possibilities you can make happen, rather than wishing and hoping something will just magically take place.

Passion happens when you are authentic, do what you love, and know deep in your soul it's what you should be doing. When your actions are in alignment with your passion, many great things happen, both personally and profession-ally. Instead of watching the clock, hoping for time to pass by quickly, you will find yourself wishing there were more hours in a day because you love what you are doing.

Living with intention and by design, rather than by de-fault or waiting for something to happen, can make your entire world change. If you aren't living with passion, you are simply existing—going through life numb, waiting, wishing, and hoping. I want to help you stop just existing and make incredible changes that will be—without trying to sound dramatic—life changing. Your dreams, goals, desires, and PASSION are waiting for you. The question really is, "Are you ready?"

The program's last module helps identify your strengths with two in-depth, detailed, and scientific assessments. These assessments identify what makes you tick and how you re-spond to things, and allows you to formulate a course of action. This is a crucial and important step that will start your journey on the right path.

Go on Your Own Journey

Without knowing where you are in your own journey, I cannot provide specifics or examples of how important this passion and purpose thing is. However, I can tell you that if you want to feel more alive, be more content, and experience life rather than just existing and dealing with it, make it NOT about you. Focus on others: helping, teaching, mentoring, loving, forgiving, and assisting.

The best way to live is to help those around you.

Be selfless with your blessings, your time, and your gifts. Use them to help others, and you will be amazed at what comes back to you.

I believe in my heart that most people can be successful. I don't believe in luck. If it happens to look like luck, I believe it's God-guided and/or a lot of hard work was behind it. Those I've interviewed have worked their tails off and they have passion. They were all persistent, and they all took advantage of the blessings that were given them. And they share their success. They give.

You can do the same thing in your life. Put your passion into action. Share. Give.

The stories you read from these amazing people offer these truths from their own experiences that may help you on your journey:

From Dan Rusanowsky

1. Learn to react to things quickly.

2. Take the crappy shift that nobody wants.

3. Take a deep breath, look them in the eye, and ask, then see what happens.

4. Just forge ahead.

5. People need people who are passionate and interested.

6. Learn a lot about the business world.

7. Being a part of something from the ground up is a very special thing.

8. Learn everything you can about the business you're in.

9. A lot of it is just getting through the grind.

10. If you do something you love every day, you'll be happy to go to work.

11. Instead of chasing the dollar, pursue what you love. The living will follow.

12. Life's all about discovering what your special talent is.

13. The journey is more important than possessions.

14. You only have a certain amount of time to pursue what you love.

15. Reflect on how lucky we are to live in America.

16. No matter how long you've been doing something, keep learning about it.

17. Find new goals every day and life will never be boring.

18. Be remembered as someone who made other people's lives happier.

From Ivan and Beth Misner

1. Diplomacy is the art of letting someone else have your way.

2. The secret to success is hard work.

3. You need patience and persistence to achieve excellence.

4. Search for your passion so you can work in your flame— and you may not know what it looks like until you try it.

5. Practice extreme focus, once you identify your passion. Don't let your attention get too divided.

From Dale Brown

1. No one will ever intimidate me or someone I love.

2. The bully is a phony.

3. It doesn't take a giant of a man to stand up.

4. Be on a quest for learning.

5. When you love what you do, it's not a job, it's a passion.

6. We are our brother's keeper. That's how we're supposed to be.

7. Actions are what we need.

8. Always lower the attention you're getting.

9. God doesn't make any junk, and that means you're more than enough.

10. Exceptional leaders help people think more of themselves.

11. You can be a weak wimp or you can get fired up.

12. If it's not real, it won't last.

13. Happiness, freedom, and peace are the three most important things in life. You cannot have them unless you're giving them to someone else.

14. It doesn't take a battalion. It takes a few people being creative.

15. The first sign of strength is gentleness.

16. The most extraordinary people on earth are the most ordinary people.

From Jamie Anderson

1. Give yourself the freedom to grow, learn, and explore nature.

2. Find opportunities to find passion for what you're interested in.

3. Seek different challenges that are intimidating and difficult to figure out. In time, you'll be able to do things you didn't even think were possible.

4. Don't have attachments or expectations.

5. Work hard to get what you want.

6. Don't get wrapped up in what other people are saying.

7. Do your best for a higher reason.

8.   Stay humble and grateful.

9.   Know, intrinsically, that you're going to win.

10. Connect your passion to your mind, body, and spirit.

11. Respect the elements.

12. We're all a part of the problem, and we're all a part of the solution.

13. Help wherever you can.

14. We need more people who are following what they love to find true balance and harmony within our globe.

15. Everything happens for a reason.

16. Get out, explore, be yourself.

17. Once you say yes, things are going to happen. Things just start working out.

18. Relax a little more. Trust and let it be.

19. You are what you make of your situation. It's all about perception.

20. Live for the moment and love what you do. Be passionate about what you do.

From Ryan Smith

1.   You can have a meaningful impact through business.

2.   Find better, innovative ways to do things.

3.   Take something complex and make it simple, easy, and usable.

4. If you fail, you might meet their expectations. If you win, you prove them all wrong.

5. Add the features people request, knowing that if you do, you'll already have a buyer.

6. Get enough distributors and channels.

7. Great trials are great processes in which to mature.

8. Explore new frontiers of efficiency and automation.

9. Develop yourself; expand your horizons.

10. It all comes down to what you think.

11. Is the purpose behind each day to get something or to give something?

12. Giving is like a boomerang. What you throw out, you get back.

13. See opportunities wherever you are.

14. The intent is more important than the result.

15. Focus on those who really need your help.

16. Seek lasting returns, not quick returns.

Acknowledgments

Thanks to my father, Ronald L. Kern, who has supported me in many of my ventures, especially when, at the time, they seemed far-fetched or too lofty. He taught me work ethic and the rewards of it, and to stick to something even when it gets rough. Thank you, Dad.

Few things in my life would have turned out so well without my wife Lisa's support. I owe so much to her that one thousand pages wouldn't be enough for me to express everything in my heart. Thank you, Lisa, my bride of more than 28 years, my "presh," and the single most important person in my life. You are my everything and I thank God daily for blessing me with you. You are my one true love, my friend, my utopia.

I also want to acknowledge my children, Heather and Tony. If it weren't for their support and love, this book never would have happened. It is my hope that this book directs them to choose what makes them happy and that they realize by doing so, the rest will fall into place.

I've had great support through personal and professional struggles from my brother, Dan Kern, and my sister, Melody Corber. They both have always been supportive and loved me, and I cherish the unique relationship that I have with both of them.

About the Author

Ronald Kern is an entrepreneur at heart. Although he was $26,000 in debt and had no formal education after high school, he founded a private investigation company in the basement of his parent's home. He and his wife, Lisa, turned it into a multimillion-dollar operation and one of the top five firms in the United States.

Ronald started and guided many successful companies in photography and videography, web design, decals, radio, and voice-over, to name a few. In 2013, Ronald and his wife, Lisa, sold all companies and "retired" to pursue other passions—including helping and educating youth. They have worked with children on the Pine Ridge Indian Reservation in South Dakota and provided school supplies to children in Roatan, Honduras. Locally, they spent a year providing food, clothing, and necessities to the homeless population in Boise. Ron and Lisa created LIMBitless, a nonprofit organization that helps combat wounded veterans and adaptive persons. In 2018, they sold their dream home and now live on a 42-acre farm and ranch where they offer cooking classes, equine therapy, farm stays, and much more.

Ronald says, "Stop comparing yourself to others as a gauge of your own self-worth. There is no such scale and you have strength, beauty, skills, dreams, ideas, value, and are loved by many. Add passion and your purpose to the mix, put it in action, and you will be unstoppable!"

Ronald is an Equine Trauma Connection Specialist and is Certified in PLT (Polychromatic Light Therapy). He is also a Certified Professional Behavior Analyst, Driving Forces Analyst, Entrepreneurship Master Coach, Leadership & Development Master Coach, Personal Success Master Coach, Certified Marketing & Social Media Coach, Certified Business Strategy & Growth Expert, Certified Go-Giver Life & Business Master Coach, and a Certified Expert in Assessments. It is his experience with turning passion into profession that fuels his desire to encourage and inspire others.

One of Ron's biggest interests and passions is studying the American Revolution and all those who were involved—both names you would recognize and many you have never heard of. Genealogy of his ancestors was part of his studies and has proven his fifth great-grandfather, Peter Kern, and Peter's two brothers served and fought in the Revolutionary War. Ron is currently working on his first historical fiction book, *Taking Up Arms: A Story of Three Brothers Who Fought Together in the American Revolution.* You can learn more by visiting www.AmericanRevolutionHistory.com

MyPassioninAction.com
Back-Forty-Farms.com
NeuroBalancedLife.com
LIMBitless.org
AmericanRevolutionHistory.com